The GOVERNOR *Reports:* 1951 - 1958

Governor THEODORE R. McKELDIN

The GOVERNOR *Reports:* 1951-1958

How Maryland met the challenge of the 1950's

1958

THE GOVERNMENT HOUSE · ANNAPOLIS, MARYLAND

Contents

Contents

Foreword

By THEODORE R. McKELDIN, *Governor*

As the first half of the Twentieth Century came to a close, Maryland was in a stage of extraordinary growth.

While most of the nation suffered similarly from post-war growing pains, this State was destined to be among the few in which population expansion would outstrip the national rate of increase for many years to come.

Maryland welcomed the challenge of the times.

Much of the growth was due to the happy circumstances of geography, with Baltimore—the State's metropolis—providing the westernmost of the nation's fine Atlantic seaports. Baltimore had played a magnificent role in production and shipping for the Second World War, and many who had come to man the plants and ships and handle the precious cargos of victory remained to be a part of expanding economy.

But Maryland had other than its natural attractions. It had a history of enterprise from the days of the clipper ships through the building of railroads and on to the days of multiple transportation by land, sea and air.

A succession of State Administrations and General Assemblies had built and maintained a well-balanced tax structure that was attractive both to industry and individual citizens.

The State was a pioneer and remained a leader in high-ranking public health services.

Fine universities and colleges, including those operated by the State and private institutions encouraged and aided by the State, maintained outstanding facilities for research and a source of enlightened manpower.

Public primary and secondary schools, operated by Baltimore City and the Counties and substantially aided from the State Treasury, were in step with the educational progress of the Nation. The State, recognizing the emergency needs for additional school buildings, had inaugurated a system of extending its excellent credit to the civil divisions when needed for school construction.

Yes, in 1951, Maryland was in step with many of her neighbors and ahead of some.

But stretching well into the distance, there remained broad avenues of opportunity for progress and improvement.

The State Government itself, in many areas, was bent by the burden of obsolescence.

A start had been made on recovery from the war-necessitated era of neglect which had been inflicted upon the State's physical plant, but the great bulk of the work remained to be planned and accomplished.

The mighty post-war upsurge of motor cars and trucks as instruments of pleasure and commerce emphasized the inadequacy of Maryland roads.

In the broad fields of public health, in Maryland as in other States, there had been an awakening to the almost medieval stagnation in our treatment of the mentally ill, and State officials were responding to the public clamor for improvement. A good start had been made on better housing and physical treatment of patients, but much more was needed and new methods of treatment and research and much of the plant to accommodate them awaited accomplishment. The good chronic disease program in which Maryland had pioneered had bogged down. Authorization for the State to engage in the systematic study and treatment of alcoholism had been written into law and forgotten.

The penal system reached out in a vain effort to grasp a hard hold on the fast moving century.

On January 10, 1951, as a newly inaugurated Governor, I promised to approach the problem of governmental obsolescence by giving "effect now to the mandate of the 1947 Legislature for the appointment of a commission on the reorganization of the State Government and its Departments."

A major objective, I said, "would be . . . to improve the State's fiscal policies."

In the same inaugural address, I promised: "An Advisory Council on Highway Construction . . . to review promptly the State's road building program."

"The humane duty we owe to the mentally sick, the tubercular and the chronically ill, the aged and the indigent in all recognized categories," I told my inaugural audience, "must continue as a compelling obligation of the State."

From time to time, other study commissions were appointed to report to me and to the General Assembly—one that revised the formula under which the State bears its share of teachers' salaries, resulting in general increases—one which continues active devising improvements in many areas of the government.

Meanwhile, we have proceeded with the constant improvement of our physical plant—our University, our State Colleges, our Teachers Colleges, our Training Schools and our Hospitals.

We have built and are occupying a new State Office Building in Annapolis, and, as this is written, another is nearing completion in Baltimore. The latter will bring together under one roof most of the long-scattered departments of the State Government which have been occupying expensive rented space throughout the City.

Entirely aside from the long-range roads program was our planning and building of the tunnel under Baltimore harbor, a major step in relieving the awful traffic congestion in Baltimore's rush hours.

Indeed, the loyal men and women throughout the State Government have been in step with the times and the progress of the future, and accomplishment has been the rule in all departments.

Noting the approach to the close of my second term—the limit allowed under our Constitution—I called upon each Department and Agency head to render a concise report to me, so that I could report to you—the taxpayers of Maryland.

This is in recognition of your right to know what your tax dollars have bought. It should serve, too, to make you aware that progress is a continuing thing—that in the course of government, there is no resting place.

I proudly present to you the reports that you will find in the following pages. I urge that they be read with care. I hope they will serve to further arouse your interest in government—for your interest and concern are essential to a government of popular sovereignty.

Commission on Administrative Organization

Since its inception in September, 1953, this Commission submitted eleven reports. Outlined below are résumés of each report defining its studies and recommendations and end results.

MARYLAND BUDGET SYSTEM

The report recommended major improvements in the State's budget system including a constitutional amendment, ratified by the voters in 1952, to permit adoption of the program form of budget. Other innovations resulting from this report were: the "one-package budget" a comprehensive fiscal program setting forth at one time the Governor's entire fiscal program; the rigid restriction of the use of supplemental budgets; expansion of the Budget Bureau to increase the effectiveness of its services to the State departments and the Governor; a system of inventory controls; and creation of a Central Payroll Bureau. Some of these changes required legislative approval; others were implemented only by executive action.

LOCAL LEGISLATION

This Review dealt with the General Assembly's problem in considering and acting on matters of State-wide importance when the legislative machinery is jammed with huge volumes of local legislation for each of the 150 municipalities and 23 counties. The Commission felt that wider exercise of legislative functions by the subdivisions was the only logical and practical solution to the problem faced by the General Assembly and that this would strengthen democratic processes and effective administration at the local level. The Legislature adopted and the people ratified a constitutional amendment giving home rule to Maryland's incorporated municipalities by authorizing them to amend their own charters and providing that, except for legislation on tax rate and debt limits, the General Assembly shall enact only general legislation applicable to all municipalities within a given classification.

STATE-LOCAL FISCAL RELATIONS

Study reviewed the problems of the pyramiding of taxes at the Federal, State and local levels. The Commission recommended and the Legislature adopted a policy that no municipality share in State revenue unless it raises a minimum amount of revenue locally. The General Assembly passed legislation recommended by the Commission to improve the financial reports rendered by local governments to the State.

HIGHWAY RELATIONSHIPS

This report dealt mainly with improvement in administrative relationships between State, county and municipal highway authorities. Many of these required no legislation. The legislative recommendations were for reclassification of highways, highway statute revision, and provision for coordinated long-range planning at all levels of government.

INDUSTRIAL RELATIONS AND SAFETY

The Commission made recommendations, adopted by the General Assembly, for centralizing in one agency the safety programs now dispersed among a number of departments. Centralization should result in improved service at no greater cost to taxpayers. The Commission's recommendations for separation of administrative functions from the quasi-judicial functions of the Employment Security Board have been adopted.

HEALTH AND WELFARE ADMINISTRATION

This study discussed the Department of Health, Department of Mental Hygiene, Water Pollution Control Commission, Miners Hospital, Department of Public Welfare and the Maryland Veterans Commission. The major part of this report reviews the structure of the Health and Welfare departments and their organizational and fiscal relations with the counties. In accordance with Commission recommendations the Governor appointed a Committee to formulate a plan for equitable allocation of the financial burden of the public health service between the State and the counties. The plan was duly submitted and adopted. The Commission's recommendation for transfer of Miners Hospital to local control and operation was approved and a program of gradual withdrawal by the State, satisfactory to both State and local interests is now in process. The transition will be completed by July 1, 1961.

REGULATORY ADMINISTRATION

This review dealt with a matter of primary concern to citizens whose activities are increasingly affected by the operations of quasi-judicial regulatory authorities and licensing agencies. Maryland has 23 occupational licensing boards and fifteen agencies regulating labor and business. The State has adopted the Commission's recommendation for an administrative procedure act establishing fundamental principles to make sure that administrative agencies are subject to essential controls but are not unduly hampered in the performance of their functions. This act makes uniform provisions as to rule-making powers, declaratory judgments, administrative hearings of an adjudicatory nature and judicial review of administrative decisions.

PUBLIC WORKS ADMINISTRATION

This report called for better administrative relationships among agencies involved in planning and execution of capital improvements. These recommendations have been adopted. Considerable benefit will accrue from the General Assembly's adoption of the Commission's recommendations: to restrict the use of funds secured from sale of bonds to capital improvements of a long-term nature commenced promptly after authorized; to apply unexpended bond funds to the reduction of the State debt; and to prevent the initiation of any project that cannot be completed within the amount authorized for it.

PERSONNEL ADMINISTRATION

This study reviewed the operation of the merit system. The basic system was deemed sound and a number of administrative suggestions were made, several of which already have been adopted. The Legislature adopted Commission recommendations reorganizing the Standard Salary Board, providing for the removal under certain conditions, of names of persons from eligible lists for positions, and changing the title of the State Employment Commission to "Commissioner of Personnel."

CORRECTION AND PAROLE ADMINISTRATION

This report resulted in wide-sweeping changes in penal administration. The Commission recommended, and the General Assembly passed a law separating the policy-making functions of the Board of Correction from the administrative and transferring the latter to the Superintendent of Prisons. Other procedural and administrative changes were adopted.

The Commission's comprehensive review of parole activity resulted in recommendations: (1) to create a Board of Parole and Probation; (2) to take away from the Governor the duty of taking final action on parole recommendations; (3) to give the new Board authority to grant or revoke paroles, discharge from parole supervision or rescind such action; and (4) to make the Chairman of the new Board an ex officio member of the Board of Correction. These recommendations were adopted by the General Assembly with the modification to provide that the Governor must continue to act on paroles of prisoners serving life terms. The effect of adopting the Commission's recommendations is that prisoners are considered more promptly for parole, better supervision is granted parolees, offenders have greater chance for rehabilitation, prison crowding is relieved and the tax burden for penal administration is lessened.

ADMINISTRATION OF JUVENILE DELINQUENCY CONTROL

This study found many inadequacies in the administration of the training school program for delinquents and concluded that they were due in large part to confusion of authority between the Department of Public Welfare and the individual Boards of Managers of the four schools. The 1953 General Assembly clarified the role of the Welfare Department as the central administrative agency responsible for the program. The Governor's 1955 fiscal year budget provided for implementation of the Department's responsibilities for providing delinquency prevention services and for rehabilitating young people and in the subsequent year a forestry camp program was inaugurated. The problem is complex and far from solution, but much has been done to carry out the Commission's numerous recommendations to improve the effectiveness of the State's services in preventing and treating delinquency.

State Roads Commission

The rapid rise in construction of sorely needed highways in Maryland since the close of World War II has resulted in wide and rapid expansion of the functions of the State Roads Commission.

The Commission, in 1958, completed 50 years of continuous service. It is one of the oldest administrative bodies in the State.

When the history of the Twentieth Century is written, it will contain no chapter more graphic than that of the struggle of the road builders to keep abreast of the auto makers.

Maryland met the problem head-on at mid-century.

The State Administration in 1951 launched an eighteen-month survey under the State Roads Commission which produced some astounding figures. On the 4,736 miles of State roads were found:

6,700 curves too sharp for normal driving speed.

12,800 places where hills, hollows, curves or obstructions limit view of the road ahead to less-than-safe distances at normal driving speed.

1,900 hills long enough and steep enough to slow down heavy vehicles and produce the creeping congestion that tempts impatient drivers to take dangerous chances.

In order to bring Maryland's highways up to modern standards of safety and to cope with ever-increasing traffic, it was found that we must rebuild 3,150 miles and construct an additional 300 miles on new locations.

This was the genesis of Maryland's 12-year road program, passed by the Legislature of 1953 and launched the following year. It was unique in that it set up a long-term schedule on a priority basis, with definite but flexible mileage improvements allocated each county in each four-year period.

PLANNING ACCLAIMED

It has been acclaimed as an excellent piece of highway planning. It has twice won the "golden milestone" award for excellence in highway programming and performance, an accolade bestowed bi-annually by the National Highway Users Conference. Only one other state has twice won that award.

Definite results of this farsighted road planning now are visible.

One of the most beautiful highways in the country is the Washington National Pike, built from the city of Frederick south to the National Capital. It has been completed as far south as Rockville.

Another is the Baltimore-Washington Expressway. A third is the Baltimore-Harrisburg Expressway, rolling northward from Baltimore to an ultimate junction with the Pennsylvania road system at the Mason-Dixon Line. In 1956 the State opened another super-highway, the Blue Star Memorial, crossing the Eastern Shore for a length of 48 miles from the Delaware line west to the Chesapeake Bay Bridge, which was opened to traffic in 1952.

A most important project, from both the safety and the expediting of traffic, was the relocation of U. S. Route 40 over Martin's and Polish mountains in Western Maryland. The deepest road cut in the state, perhaps in the East, is that of 147 feet that was excavated on Polish mountain.

The most spectacular project of the eight-year period was the building of the Baltimore Harbor Tunnel-Expressway system, a quick and effective route to and through the State's chief city. This was Maryland's largest public project, built at a cost of some $130,000,000 and financed entirely by toll bonds. It was opened to traffic in November, 1957. It was built by the Commission and is operated under a toll-facility division which also manages the Chesapeake Bay, Susquehanna River and Potomac River Bridges.

However, the roads program was not at all centered upon super-highways. The majority of the improved mileage is on secondary roads, known as "farm to market" or "home to office" roads.

To sum up, during the first four years of the program (1954-1957

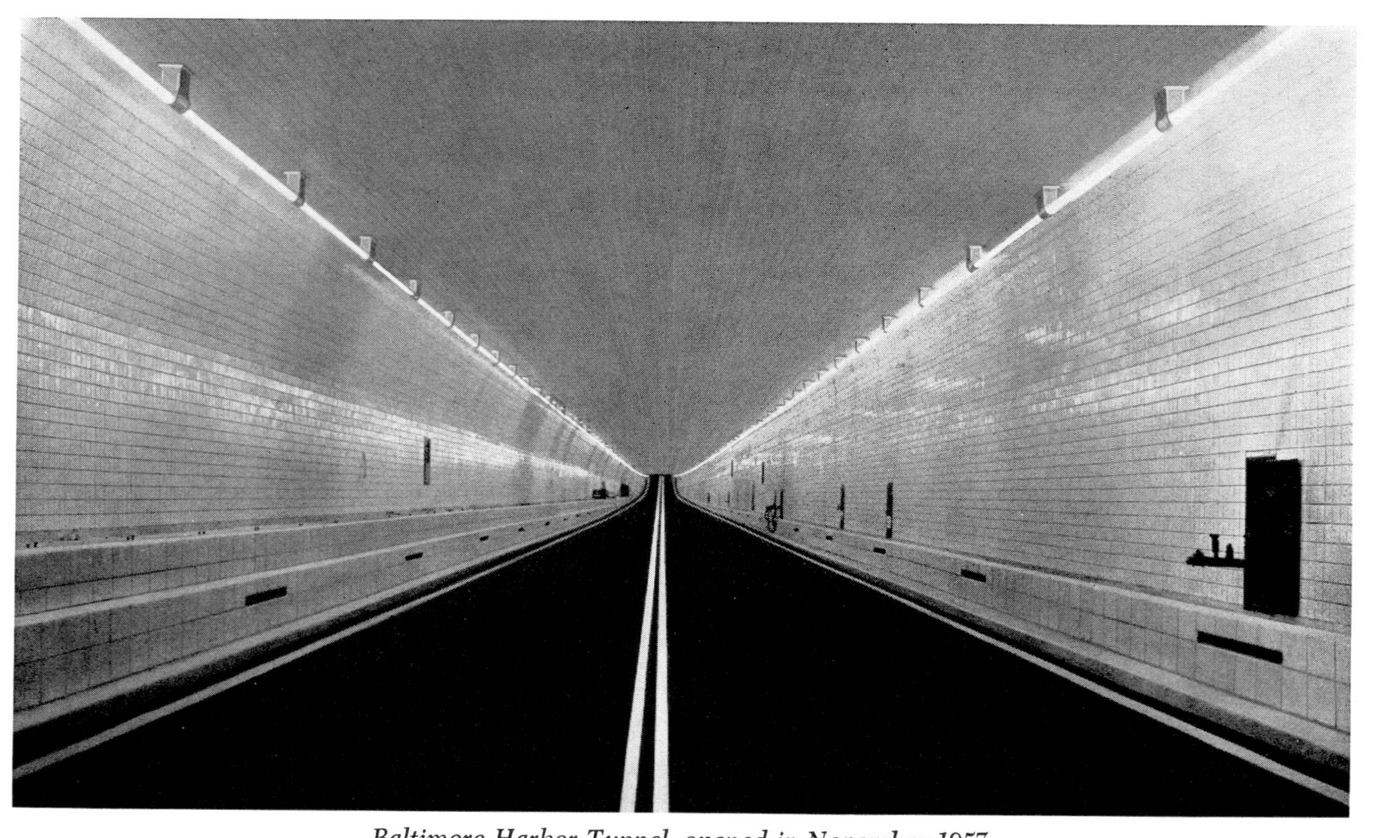

Baltimore Harbor Tunnel, opened in November 1957.

inclusive) a total of 888 miles of new or reconstructed roads was completed, advertised or put under contract at a cost of $276,894,000.

FEDERAL AID FUNDS

The State program was supplemented in 1956 by the Federal Interstate Highway Act, a long-range plan of controlled access roads linking the principal cities of the nation.

Under the interstate system Maryland was allocated 353 miles of highways to be built or rebuilt to "interstate standards," meaning full access control (no traffic lights and no grade crossings). The federal act provides that 90 per cent of the cost is paid by the federal government and 10 per cent by the States.

The exact amount which Maryland will receive from this federal fund is unknown. It is dependent upon many factors including congressional formulas, emergency federal legislation and the fluctuating state of the Federal Highway Trust Fund. Maryland is ready to utilize every penny allocated to it by the federal government. Maryland was the first state in the nation to "cover" its 1957 and 1958 allocation of funds; that is, submit detailed plans and specifications acceptable to the Federal Bureau of Public Roads and place the projects under contract. During 1956, 1957 and 1958 Maryland was allocated some $56,000,000, of which about $4,000,000 in turn was made available to the City of Baltimore for its Jones Falls Expressway. Of the $52,000,000 remaining, $47,200,000, covering 35 miles of new expressways, was under contract by early 1958. Two other projects already programmed would more than exhaust the remaining $4,800,000 in the allocation. These are a section of the Northeastern Expressway from the City line north to the Baltimore Beltway and a section of the Beltway from Belair Road (U. S. 1) eastward to the Northeastern Expressway.

The federal program superimposed on the already expanded State construction plan brought many new problems to the Commission. Faced with a vast new workload, the Commission met the challenge by (a) an internal reorganization designed to tighten up administrative procedures, (b) the use of consulting engineering firms because of the stepped-up roads program (this was done long before the advent of the 1956 Federal Interstate Highway Act), and (c) the adaptation of modern science to the new program.

For example, the Commission now is building roads for which the entire design and preliminary plans were made by aerial photography. One cameraman in an airplane is doing the work of many men in the field. The Rising Sun by-pass, opened in 1957, is an example of such a highway. The Commission has installed a Univac Electronic Computer in its road design division. Excavation computations may be made electronically

30 times faster than by manual methods and at only 10 per cent of the cost. The machines also may be used for survey computations, grade calculations and bridge designs with other fields available in future development, including traffic problems (where one hour of traffic flow can be simulated on a computer in 40 seconds) and use by the accounting division.

LEADS IN TRAINING PERSONNEL

The Roads Commission has been a pioneer in the training of its own men. It established an engineering school in 1954 in cooperation with the University of Maryland and embarked on an effort to provide pre-professional engineering training for employees who had not completed an engineering course in college. After three years, thirteen men graduated from this course in the spring of 1957 and received "Advanced Certificates in Highway Engineering." Commission engineers have been active in the joint Highway Engineering Research group at the University of Maryland. A joint project between the Commission and the Johns Hopkins University has made studies of drainage conditions, stabilization of swamp areas and the effectiveness of various types of guard rails and culverts.

In 1957-58 the Commission launched one of its most elaborate and painstaking projects, a "sufficiency study" which examined and evaluated the condition and capacity of each mile of highway on the State system. Those ratings were submitted to the Legislature in the 1958 session as part of the Roads Commission's report to that body. They also serve as the basis of a continuous "needs study" useful in determining priority allocation of improvements. Under legislation adopted by the 1958 session of the General Assembly, the Roads Commission was authorized to substitute projects in the Sufficiency Rating Report for those included in the 12-year program, thus furnishing a desirable degree of flexibility in that program.

An interesting development of the last few years has been the Roads Commission's building of asphalt groins, or jetties, to protect the beach from Ocean City northward to the Delaware line. The experiment with asphalt groins has been found to be not only less expensive but the first extensive use of such material in the country. Engineers from far and wide, including parties from Holland and other foreign countries, have come to Maryland to inspect this installation.

NEW DEVELOPMENTS

Other developments and improvements in Roads Commission technique during the eight-year period might be listed as follows: Reorganization of the Right of Way Department; development and use of dense graded base courses for highway construction to assure full usage of local materials; revision of procedures and contract items in order to insure prompt final payments to contractors; revised and greatly strengthened pre-qualification of bidders to insure more uniform practice and to assure the State of capable bidders; and the publication of a Maryland traffic control manual.

A closer liaison has been developed between the Commission, County Commissioners and members of the General Assembly, which has proved highly desirable from the standpoint of both the State and the county highway systems.

No account of Roads Commission activities would be complete without a reference to the development of the picnic area program. Since 1951, the Roads Commission has built one hundred such areas adjacent to, but completely off, State highways. These sites, each containing picnic tables, benches, fireplaces and parking spaces, are made use of by more than 500,000 people each year.

In 1958 the Legislature passed a bill sponsored by the Roads Commission prohibiting billboards and other advertising signs within 600 feet of Expressways. Although anti-billboard measures have been before the General Assembly for many years, this was the first enactment of a bill to give real protection to the State's huge investment in limited access highways such as the Baltimore-Harrisburg Expressway, the Baltimore-Washington Expressway, the Washington National Pike and others. It was designed to "give Maryland scenery a chance to be seen."

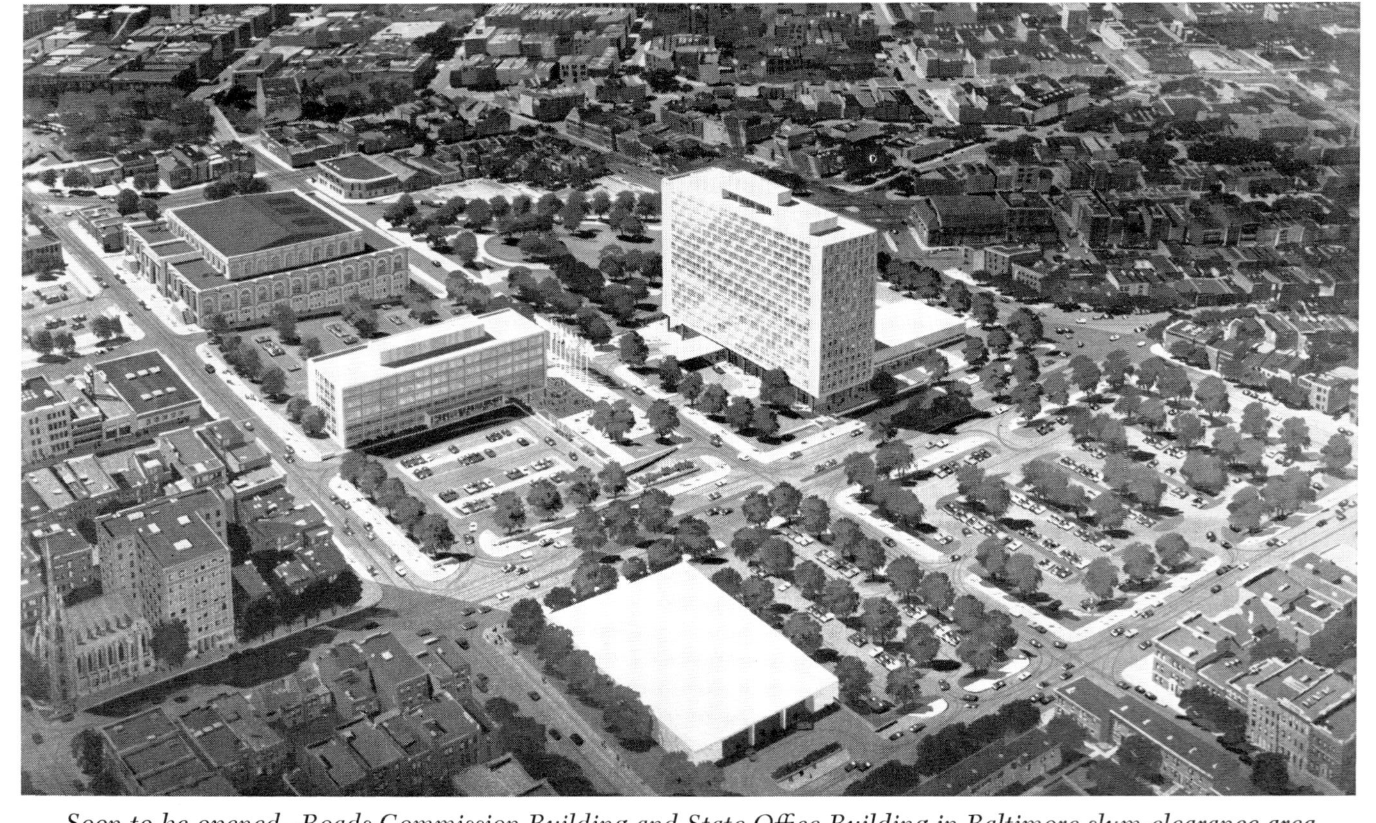

Soon to be opened—Roads Commission Building and State Office Building in Baltimore slum-clearance area.

Department of Public Improvements

The Department of Public Improvements, established by the General Assembly to provide technical assistance and advice to the Board of Public Works in connection with all phases of State construction excepting roads and bridges, has from 1951 through 1957, supervised expenditures, totalling slightly over $100,000,000. This figure includes new construction, renovation and expansion of existing facilities, and architectural and engineering fees on major projects.

Notable among the accomplishments during this period have been the actual establishment of the following entirely new institutions or facilities.

PATUXENT INSTITUTION

In 1952 construction was begun for the totally new Institution for Defective Delinquents, later named Patuxent Institution. First stage construction was completed near the end of 1954, providing a functional unit with a capacity of approximately 400, complete with heating plant. More recently there has been completed an auditorium-vocational training building, and now ready to go under contract is a dining-hall-kitchen building to replace the temporary facilities presently located in the main building. Currently in the planning stage, with contract award expected before the end of 1958, is a $2,000,000 diagnostic center to provide complete diagnostic facilities for this institution.

MONTEBELLO STATE HOSPITAL

In 1952 the State purchased from the City of Baltimore the buildings and grounds of the former Sydenham Hospital which had been operated by the City as a communicable disease hospital. The purpose of this purchase was to establish under the operation of the State Department of Health a chronic disease hospital to serve the Baltimore area. The property included approximately 31 acres with eight buildings. Contracts for alterations and renovations were completed in time for opening with a capacity of 142 patients in April 1953. Since that time two major new buildings have been constructed providing additional capacity for 391 patients. This new hospital provides facilities for diagnosis and various types of therapy, as well as surgery.

WESTERN MARYLAND STATE HOSPITAL

Western Maryland State Hospital is a completely new institution located on the outskirts of Hagerstown on a site donated to the State by Washington County. This 300 bed hospital includes a medical and diagnostic unit, a tuberculosis unit, as well as nursing units for ambulatory and semi-ambulatory patients. Related services provided by the institution are diagnostic X-ray, clinical laboratory, occupational and clinical therapy, as well as dental and eye clinics. This new hospital was completed in the spring of 1957. At the present time additional construction work is in progress to provide living quarters for staff personnel for this chronic disease hospital.

STATE OFFICE BUILDINGS

Currently nearing completion is a new office building for State agencies in Baltimore. A new Annapolis Office Building was completed and occupied in August, 1958. An additional tract of approximately 4.3 acres across the street from the new building provides parking facilities.

The office building construction in Baltimore consists of a fifteen story main building to house approximately forty-five state agencies currently located in rented space scattered throughout the City, and a six story plus basement building to house the offices of the State Roads Commission. The State Roads Building will house the approximately 650 employees working in the offices of that agency, while the main building will provide working quarters for approximately 1200 employees. The fifteen acre site will contain parking areas for approximately 800 automobiles. Construction of the two buildings is approximately $13,400,000.

INSTITUTION FOR CRIMINALLY INSANE

This institution, although of necessity designed as a maximum security custodial operation, has as its prime function the treatment of mentally ill, therefore the institution is to be operated by the Department of Mental Hygiene. It is a completely new institution including heating plant and all other utilities, as well as the patient buildings, constructed on a site at Jessups transferred from the ownership of the Department of Correction to the Department of Mental Hygiene. Funds for the first stage construction of this institution were included in the Capital Improvement Program of 1953, and contract for a functional institution designed for this specific purpose to accommodate approximately 300 patients was awarded in 1957. Additional construction to complete the program for this institution was authorized by the 1958 General Assembly.

LONG TERM CARE COLONY

This is another completely new institution to be operated by the Department of Mental Hygiene designed for the care of adult feeble-minded patients who are not mental cases but do require custodial care. There are approximately 1200 such patients currently occupying facilities of the mental hospitals only because previously there had been no other accommodation for them.

In designing a self-contained colony for this group, located on property of Rosewood State Training School, it was possible to provide much more economical construction than that necessary for the care and treatment of mental cases. Construction of this specifically designed building to accommodate 400 such patients reflected costs of less than $2,300 per bed, whereas costs for construction of patient buildings to house various types of mental cases have ranged from $5,000 to $10,000 per bed. This will make possible the removal of patients from Spring Grove's Old Center Building, and the abandonment of this building, parts of which are over 100 years old.

COPPIN STATE TEACHERS COLLEGE

Formerly located on the third floor of an elementary school in Baltimore and operated by the City of Baltimore, this school was integrated into the State Teachers College System after the close of the school year in 1950. The facilities were entirely inadequate, and with the broadening of its objectives under State operation to train teachers for elementary schools throughout the State, the property at 2500 W. North Avenue in Baltimore, formerly operated as the Lutheran Deaconess' Home, was purchased early in 1952.

The property consisted of approximately 11 acres and was improved by a main building constructed of granite containing approximately 92,000 sq. ft., with modern heating plant in three floors and basement. In addition there are four residence type structures on the property. Contract was immediately awarded for accomplishing renovations and the necessary alterations, and was completed so that the school could occupy its new quarters for the fall 1952 semester.

NEW CONSTRUCTION AT EXISTING INSTITUTIONS

Many other contracts have been completed for new construction at existing institutions including patient facilities for approximately 700 at the mental institutions alone. New construction at State schools, colleges and for the University has been highlighted by the construction of seven new libraries and major additions to the library at Morgan State College.

Construction will begin very soon on a new medical library for the

University Medical School in Baltimore. Construction of these new libraries had become desirable and necessary to keep pace with the growth and requirements of the schools. In most cases the space formerly occupied has been converted into classrooms and laboratories to aid in relieving the pressures on those facilities.

For the Military Department complete new National Guard Armories have been constructed at Catonsville, Annapolis and Salisbury and a program for the renovation, modernization and expansion of the National Guard Armories throughout the State has been carried out.

To meet the growing requirements of penal institutions and training schools, construction of new facilities in those areas has been continued throughout the years of this administration.

All additional construction at any existing institution creates additional load requirements on heating systems, water supply, sewerage, electrical supply and distribution, roads, walks and site improvements. This effect must be calculated by the Department of Public Improvements and funds requested for the necessary expansion of such facilities so that they are available at the time of completion of new buildings. In this connection it may be noted that the state building program has in the present administration alone, included major expansion of central heating plants at twenty-one institutions. Similar expansion has been undertaken in all other utility systems.

Maryland Port Authority

The Maryland Port Authority was created in 1956 by an Act of the Maryland General Assembly. It became effective on June 1 of that year. The new agency is administered by five citizens of Maryland appointed by the Governor on a geographical basis.

Briefly, the Authority is charged with (1) improving the physical port facilities of the State, (2) the protection and enhancement of advantages of the ports of the State, and (3) the development of trade and promotion of maritime businesses.

FINANCING—PORT FACILITIES

The Maryland Port Authority is authorized to issue $15 million in special obligation bonds secured by the credit of the State. Further, the Authority is authorized to issue revenue bonds in an unlimited amount secured by revenues of the facilities to be constructed.

PORT DEVELOPMENT PROGRESS

In view of the general recognition of need for new pier construction at the Port, the physical development program has been given priority in the Authority's over-all program.

Members of the staff have contacted the owners of waterfront facilities and have conferred on plans for port development for the purpose of obtaining full cooperation from private industry and eliminating any possibility of conflict with pier construction programs of private operators. The location of desirable pier sites has been established through two complete engineering studies carried out by Knappen, Tippetts and Abbett in 1949 and 1954, conferences with port interests and considerable research work by the Authority's staff.

Recognizing both legislative intent and the needs of the Port of Baltimore for new or renovated general cargo facilities, as opposed to bulk facilities which, for the most part, are of modern design and sufficient capacity, and also recognizing the limitations of available methods of financing, the Authority has concentrated on a program of general cargo pier development in the Port.

This program includes not only suitable sites, but also schematic layouts for new facilities at each site and comparative cost estimates for construction in the various suitable areas of the Port.

Layouts and comparative cost estimates are based upon the most modern criteria for general cargo marine terminals. These criteria provide for piers to accommodate the larger general cargo vessels in use today and those contemplated in the foreseeable future. Wide slips, long berths, wide aprons and large transit shed areas, completely accessible by both truck and rail, are aimed at obtaining maximum operational efficiency through full utilization of modern-day packaging, handling and transporting methods. All dimensions are viewed as sufficiently liberal to obtain structures which will provide maximum flexibility to meet the varied and changing conditions inherent in general cargo commerce.

Based upon this survey, plans and costs of recent pier construction at this and other ports, and upon field reconnaissance, nine potential sites have been selected. Working with this information, including the estimated construction costs, the Authority has conferred with potential operators, and it appears that at least two of these sites will be developed on a self-amortizing basis.

HARBOR FIELD AS A MARINE TERMINAL

Since December 1956, negotiations and studies have also been underway to ascertain the suitability and availability of Harbor Field as a site for development of a specialized marine terminal. The studies indicate that Harbor Field has the potential for development as a major marine terminal, and this site is expected to play an important part in bettering cargo facilities of the Port and also in providing facilities to meet the special requirements of lift-on-lift-off type of handling.

PROGRESS IN DEVELOPMENT IN OTHER AREAS

The Authority has not confined its consideration to new development to the metropolitan area of Baltimore, but has moved to assist in construction of new facilities in other areas of the State. At present, the Authority is negotiating with the City of Crisfield for the provision of a large commercial and pleasure boat basin in Somer's Cove, located in that City.

The Authority has also been actively assisting business firms interested in obtaining waterfront locations, storage facilities and pier space within the State. Representatives of large businesses have been escorted around the various waterfronts and put in contact with owners of properties believed suitable for their needs. Possible Port Authority assistance in constructing waterfront facilities for industry have been the subject of numerous conferences.

NEGOTIATIONS WITH THE CITY OF BALTIMORE

The Authority has conferred with Baltimore City officials relative to carrying out the provisions of the State Legislature directing the Authority to negotiate terms and conditions whereby certain City-owned properties on the Baltimore waterfront and City-performed functions would be assigned to the Authority. These negotiations have been successfully concluded with an agreement whereby the Authority will take title to the McComas Street Terminal of the Western Maryland Railway; the National Gypsum Company pier; and the Recreation Pier as soon as bonded indebtedness against these facilities have been retired. The City will turn over to the Authority income from these facilities over and above that required to retire bonded indebtedness. The Authority in turn has assumed certain functions and responsibilities previously performed by the Bureau of Harbors of the City. These include operation of the marine radio stations, maintenance dredging, ice breaking, oil skimming, harbor scavenging, issuance of waterfront permits and similar maritime functions.

PROTECTION, ENHANCEMENT OF THE PORT'S ADVANTAGES

The Authority, in connection with private business interests, is conducting a vigorous defense of the favorable rail differential position enjoyed by the Port of Baltimore. This work is of the greatest importance to the over-all economy of the State and the Authority is extending every effort to preserve the Port's advantages.

TRADE DEVELOPMENT

The three field offices of the Export-Import Bureau of the Baltimore Association of Commerce located in New York, Chicago and Pittsburgh were taken over as the nucleus of the Authority's trade development program. In December, 1956, the Authority assumed responsibility for these offices.

The Authority has completed a study of competitive ports on the Atlantic and Gulf Coasts. Personal visits were made to the major competitive centers where promotional and advertising programs, field office administration and trade development policies were studied. Contacts with other port officials throughout the Eastern United States were established which have proved valuable in working out common problems.

Foreign trade conferences in major cities in the East and as far west as the Mississippi have been attended and participated in by staff members. Successful Maryland Port Authority functions have been held for shippers at such key points as New York, Chicago, Pittsburgh and Cleveland.

The Authority undertook the study of port promotional publications and has published and issued the "1957 Port of Baltimore Handbook," monthly "Sailing Schedule," "Port Directory," monthly "Bulletin" and "Harbor Guide."

An advertising program has been developed and promotional material with continuity and appeal has been produced with the help of a competent professional staff.

This promotion and solicitation program is receiving continuing attention with the view of developing and adopting the best program possible.

OUTLOOK

The Authority has the greatest faith in the future of the Port of Baltimore as one of the great maritime centers of the world. It has plans for constructing in this Port new cargo facilities that will be second to none in this country or abroad. In addition, efforts are being made to assist in developing the smaller ports of the State so that the economy of the various port areas will be enhanced.

Maryland State Planning Commission

During the period 1951-1958, notable progress was made in the programs of the State Planning Commission undertaken to carry out its major responsibilities. The Commission has for the past several years prepared the State's Long-Term Capital Improvement Program on an annual rather than on the previous biennial basis. In this task, the Commission has closely followed the progress of State agencies, studied their programs and needs, and recommended each year those proposed projects which are essential to the carrying out of agency functions and appear to be of the greatest urgency. On-site inspection of facilities, staff research, studies by the Committee on Medical Care, and close teamwork with the Department of Public Improvements and the Department of Budget and Procurement have contributed importantly to the development of carefully planned programs of capital improvements.

In a period of rapidly growing population and greatly expanded State services, capital improvement needs have been met without impairing the long-standing "AAA" credit rating of the State.

SPECIAL 1957 STUDY

In order to hold in bounds the ever-mounting demands for staff housing units, the Commission undertook a special study and in early 1957 adopted a policy with respect to employee housing facilities at State institutions. The policy limits the purposes for which such projects may qualify for approval, the types of accommodations and construction costs, and the furnishing of such units. A companion study of student dormitory facilities at State-supported institutions of higher learning has led to a better screening of proposed projects, including limitation of construction costs.

During the past several years continual refinement and strengthening of the Commission's capital improvement programming process has been accomplished; the definition of projects which qualify as a capital improvement, the development of a series of planning instructions and the provision of advance planning funds to provide for the preparation of preliminary plans for major building projects. Further strengthening of capital improvement programming is expected to result from a recent legislative directive requiring each of the State departments and institutions to prepare a 10-year development program. These programs are to be submitted to the Commission not later than July 1, 1959, and will be used in evaluating all future capital project requests.

GENERAL STATE, REGIONAL AND LOCAL PLANNING

The Commission prepared and submitted to the Governor and General Assembly in 1952 a State-wide master plan for recreation and parks. Based upon a systematic expansion of State facilities, the plan called for eight parks, ten recreation reserves, ten picnic areas, and six historic reserves.

Regional studies carried out by the Commission during the period included: an effective land-use program for the Monocacy Watershed, covering 742 square miles in Frederick, Carroll and Montgomery Counties; a program for the development of recreational assets in Western Maryland as a means of increasing the level of employment and income in the region and a plan for the economic development of Denton and Caroline Counties. As an aid to counties and municipalities interested in expanding industrial payrolls, the Commission published a "Handbook of Procedure on Organizing for Industrial Development." Two studies, "Lonaconing—An Economic Survey," published in 1956, and "Economic Base and Prospects, Pocomoke City, Maryland," published in 1957, indicate the continuing assistance which the Commission is rendering to local communities.

Serving increasingly as a clearing house on planning and zoning procedures, the Commission has provided county and municipal planning agencies with technical advice on the preparation of proposals for federal aid for planning studies, the development of community plans, the enforcement of zoning and subdivision regulations, and the implementation of local capital improvement programs. Programs have been prepared to provide master plans for Salisbury and Rockville, and the Commission has submitted applications for Federal Urban Planning Assistance Grants to carry out these projects.

To fill a broad gap in basic data pertaining to Maryland's population and economic base, the Commission in 1953 issued population forecasts through 1970 for each of the counties and cities in the State and in 1954 issued a series of income estimates for the 23 counties and Baltimore City.

In addition, the Commission has published the results of its economic research dealing with the growth of manufactures in Maryland, location factors in establishing new manufacturing firms, manufacturers' tax exemptions, residential development in Baltimore City and Baltimore County, and the economic importance of port-linked manufacturing in the Baltimore Metropolitan Area. The Commission publishes a monthly Newsletter reporting on economic developments as they affect the counties and the State as a whole and maintains a current inventory of vacant industrial plants in Maryland. These statistical and economic research activities have not only contributed importantly to State and local planning, but also have provided valuable assistance to out-of-State firms seeking new locations in Maryland.

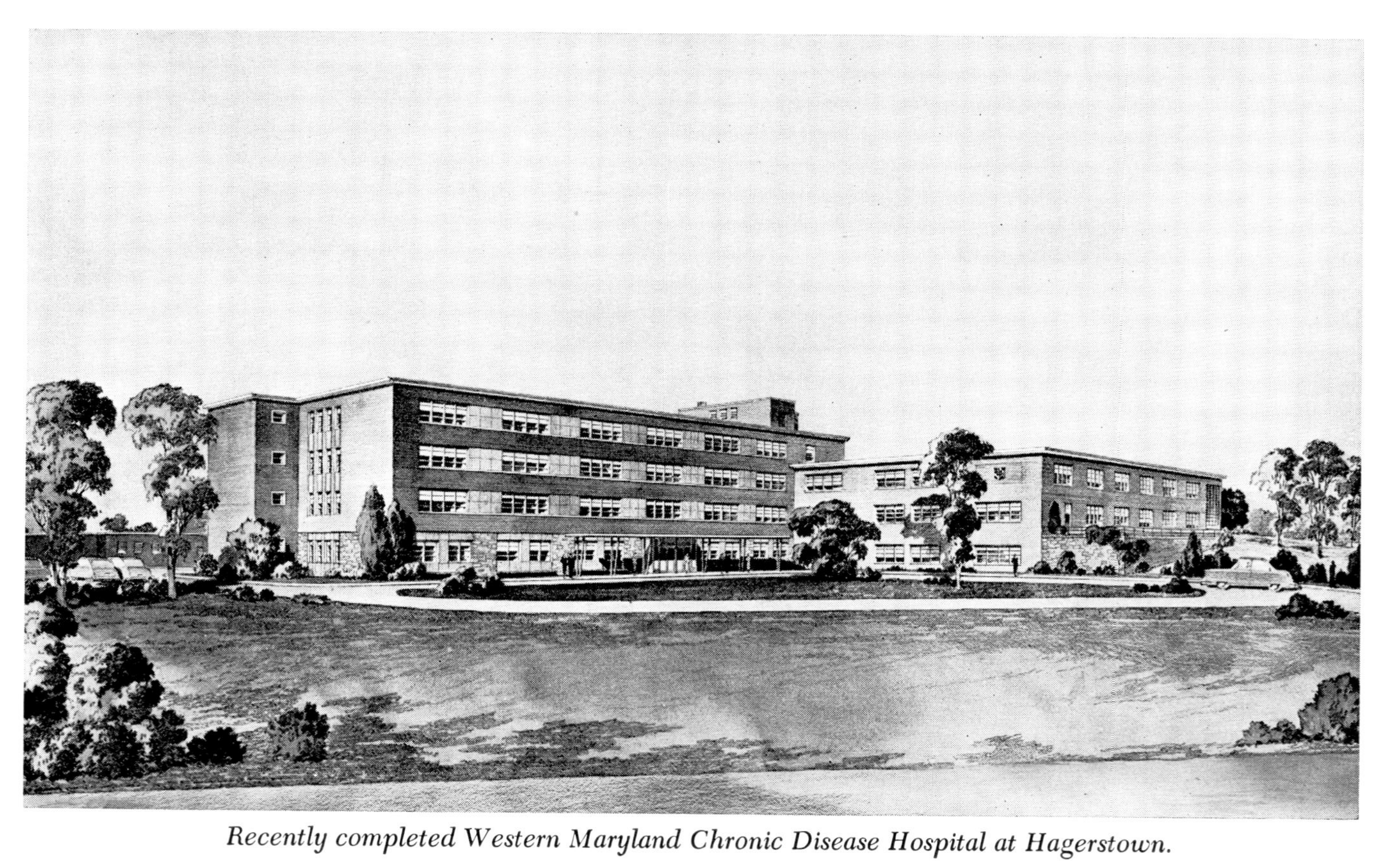

Recently completed Western Maryland Chronic Disease Hospital at Hagerstown.

BALTIMORE REGIONAL PLANNING COUNCIL

In June 1957, the Baltimore Regional Planning Council commenced operations with a federal grant under Section 701 of the National Housing Act of 1954. The Council—an "ad hoc" group consisting of two representatives each from Baltimore City and Anne Arundel, Baltimore, Carroll, Harford and Howard Counties, with the Director of the State Planning Commission as its Chairman—is charged with the responsibility of preparing a comprehensive plan for the Baltimore region based upon the following two-year studies: population, land-use, industrial development, arterial highways, water supply and sewerage facilities.

Growing out of the urgent need for a coordinated approach to regional planning problems, the project is being carried out by a small staff on its own, staff time, equivalent in total to the federal grant, is contributed by the member jurisdictions.

COMMITTEE ON MEDICAL CARE

Under a joint agreement with the Rockefeller Foundation and the Medical and Chirurgical Faculty of Maryland, the Office of Studies was established in October 1951 as the research arm of the Commission's Committee on Medical Care. In addition to conducting major studies as requested by the Governor and General Assembly, the Office of Studies has performed a valuable service in coordinating the activities of the different subcommittees of the Committee on Medical Care and in furnishing technical advice in connection with health and medical care projects in the Long-Term Capital Improvement Program.

At the request of the Governor, the Commission's Committee on Medical Care undertook to review the medical care program of the State. A subcommittee carried out a comprehensive study of the operation of the program in the counties and Baltimore City. Its finding and recommendations were transmitted to the Governor and General Assembly in February 1953.

With the cooperative effort of some fifty experts, the Subcommittee on Nursing Needs spent more than two years in an exhaustive examination of "Nursing Needs and Resources in the State of Maryland." Based on a careful analysis of the existing situation and prescribed standards to be met for adequate nursing care, the Subcommittee's program, transmitted to the Governor in May 1953, offered a highly constructive plan for improving the training, recruitment, and utilization of nursing service personnel.

In response to a request of the General Assembly, a subcommittee appointed by the Committee on Medical Care in 1953 undertook a study of the problem of public health financing, and its findings and recommendations were reported in 1955. Recently completed studies of the Committee include "Report on Diagnostic and Rehabilitation Centers for Handicapped Children," published in October 1957, and "State Grants to Aid in the Construction of Non-Profit and Public Nursing Homes," published in February 1958.

Department of Budget and Procurement

Pursuant to the submission in November, 1951, of the report of the Commission on Administrative Organization of the State on the Maryland budget system and the report of the subcommittee on purchasing procedures, this department immediately proceeded with implementing the recommendations incorporated in the reports. During fiscal 1953 the Budget Bureau concentrated its efforts in accomplishing the change from the then "line-item" budget to a recommended program or performance type budget, which, for the first time, included in one comprehensive budget all funds—General, Special, Federal and Capital Funds—collected and disbursed by the State.

The first budget under the new system for the fiscal year 1954 was presented to the 1953 regular session of the General Assembly, which received it favorably and enacted it into law. Four subsequent annual budgets, incorporating constant improvements and refinements, have been formulated, enacted and successfully administered.

The new Maryland system has received nationwide and foreign recognition and is generally considered the most progressive forward step in budgeting at State levels since our State's executive budget was adopted in 1916 as the first of the State systems of its kind.

PURCHASING STANDARDIZED

In 1952 the staff of the Purchasing Bureau started work on a three-point purchasing standardization program. The first step involving an alphabetical index of commodities has been accomplished; the second step involving the preparation of specifications for all commodities purchased is approximately 85% complete and the third step aiming at the standardization of commodities and equipment to be used is well underway.

As a result of this effort, Out-of-Schedule Requisitions for Supplies received annually, as distinguished from purchases made at regularly scheduled periods, have been reduced from 42,000 to 22,000, or almost 50%. Following the enactment of Chapter 24 of the Acts of 1952, the Purchasing Bureau, in conjunction with the State Comptroller's office and the State Auditor's office, also formulated and prescribed standards for maintaining stores and inventory control for all materials, supplies and equipment carried by State agencies.

In general, the Department of Budget and Procurement, through its dual functions of staff agency in budgetary administration, encompassing as it does innumerable and widely diversified administrative activities, and its service function of centralized purchasing, including capital program requirements, has kept pace with the growth and progress of the State through the present administration and is well prepared to meet future demands.

Department of Legislative Reference

During the years from 1951 to 1958, the Department of Legislative Reference continued and expanded its services to legislators. This work continued the pattern which had been set for the Department for more than thirty years. Perhaps the most notable accomplishment within the Department during the 1950's, therefore, was the rapid development of the Fiscal Research Bureau into an effective legislative staff agency.

The bill-drafting function of the Department continued following 1951 with little change over past years, except for a greater volume of work. In a period of four successive 90-day sessions of the General Assembly, for example, the number of bills introduced into the General Assembly increased as follows: 1951–1,268; 1953–1,499; 1955–1,492 and 1957–1,616.

In addition, the same upward trend was noticeable in the bills introduced into 30-day sessions in even years, which increased as follows: 1952–218; 1954–290; 1956–314 and 1958–323.

Although the bill-drafting work is the main function of the Department of Legislative Reference as a staff agency for the General Assembly, a number of other legislative services were developed during the 1950's. They include broader operation of the bill room, the supplying of steel post binders for bills in the third reading and the furnishing of mimeographed daily synopses of bills introduced.

One of the most valuable among the new legislative services is the mailing of advance sheets of the laws to members of the General Assembly and a wide list of other State and local officials throughout Maryland. Some 500 persons receive the advance sheets, giving them prompt and wide circulation and thereby making the laws enacted available soon after the session of the Legislature.

In 1954 the Department conducted the first orientation conference in

Maryland for newly elected members of the General Assembly. It was held in the House Chamber in the State House, Annapolis, about three weeks following the election. An entire day was spent in an intensive survey of legislative history, procedure and problems. A similar orientation conference is planned following the elections in 1958.

There is a pronounced trend all over the country for expansion of legislative staff agencies, and these developments in Maryland have been eagerly accepted by legislators and other officials.

The Fiscal Research Bureau had been created by legislation enacted in 1947 within the Department of Legislative Reference. During the period from 1951 to 1958, it has had two major fields of activity.

The first of these is to collect, tabulate and publish data on the finances of each County and incorporated town within the State. Since 1951, the Bureau has revised the forms on which local governments make their reports and also has revised the form of the report on local government finances which it publishes. Also the Bureau staff has been strengthened so that a careful check now is made of reports submitted by the various local governments in order to avoid the publication of erroneous data. As a result, it now is possible to obtain valid information concerning the fiscal affairs of the Counties and incorporated towns of the State.

The second function of the Fiscal Research Bureau is to assist any commission or committee appointed by the Governor, the General Assembly, the Legislative Council or any standing committee of the Senate or the House of Delegates to study questions of taxation and fiscal affairs. Most importantly, the Bureau also served the Legislative Council and the finance committees of the General Assembly during this period. Since 1953, the Bureau has devoted itself exclusively to serving the General Assembly, the Legislative Council and their committees, subcommittees and individual members. During the last three years, the Bureau has done much staff work in connection with the activities of the Committee on Taxation and Fiscal Matters.

The principal accomplishment of the Fiscal Research Bureau over the past seven years has been to earn a reputation as a reliable source of information with respect to the fiscal affairs of the State and its political subdivisions. The Bureau during the 1950's has contributed substantially more than ever before to the effective workings of the legislative process.

Health Department

Public health has made great strides during the past seven years and has entered a new era for improving the health of the people. Because of the advancements in the fields of medicine and science as well as improved socio-economic conditions, there has been a dramatic reduction in the incidence of communicable diseases.

The State has been free of serious epidemics and most of the communicable diseases which formerly took such a heavy toll of human lives have been substantially reduced although continuing control measures are necessary. The death rate in Maryland has reached an all-time low and the birth rate continues at a very high level.

BETTER SERVICE AT LESS EXPENSE

Among the important economy measures, devised to give the people maximum health service per dollar of expenditure, are the following:

1. Reorganization of the Department. (1951)
2. Institution of the program budget. (1953)
3. Implementation of the Case Formula method of improved and more equitable financial relationships between the State and its counties in the provision of local health services. (1956)
3. Elimination of old vital statistics registration system which is saving the counties approximately $30,000 each year. (1957)
5. Screening of State-aided patients in general hospitals to assure their placement in the lowest cost facility where their needs can be met. (1951)
6. Reduction in costs for automobile transportation and laboratory services.
7. Reduction of venereal disease clinics. (1953)
8. A method for transferring chronically ill and disabled patients from one level of care to another where the service is more appropriate for their needs and costs lower.

LOCAL HEALTH DEPARTMENTS

Health services are brought directly to the people by the twenty-three county health departments. The added impetus to local initiative and responsibility as the result of the Case Formula for financing local health services is already evident. During the past seven years eight new health centers have been built and four others have been equipped.

MATERNAL AND CHILD HEALTH SERVICES

During the past seven years the numbers of expectant mothers and children served has increased. At present approximately 10 per cent of all mothers and children in the counties receive direct health supervision through the health department.

During this same period maternal mortality has fallen approximately 60 per cent to an all-time low record.

Plans are also being worked out for better health services for mentally retarded children.

SCHOOL HEALTH SERVICES

The most dramatic activity in this field has been the widespread application of an epochal new discovery in preventive medicine—inoculation with poliomyelitis vaccine. More than half of all poliomyelitis vaccine injections to the population group, birth to 20 years and expectant mothers —more than 1,000,000 shots—were administered by the local health departments including the Baltimore City Health Department. Before the 1957 poliomyelitis season more than 75 per cent of this large and vulnerable segment of the population had received at least one injection.

CRIPPLED CHILDREN'S SERVICES

Since January 1951 there has been a 29 per cent increase in the number of children with a wide variety of handicaps for whom services have been provided by the Crippled Children's program.

Major program accomplishments include:

1. Development of services in the counties for children with epilepsy. (This was the first such program in any State health department)
2. Vision clinic services have been developed in eleven counties.
3. In cooperation with the Heart Association of Maryland, a program was launched to provide penicillin to children with rheumatic fever. The recurrence rate for those children receiving this protective medication has been cut from about 25 per cent to less than 5 per cent.
4. The Integrated Cleft Palate Clinic has been developed jointly with the Johns Hopkins Medical School and the University of Maryland Dental School.

5. Establishment in the Baltimore City Health Department of a division of handicapped children.
6. Plans were developed for the establishment of diagnostic and evaluation clinics for children with multiple handicaps at the University of Maryland and the Johns Hopkins Hospitals.

DENTAL HEALTH

During the past seven years communities have added flourine to the public water supplies so that now over 65 per cent of the total Maryland population is using water to which fluorides have been added to prevent dental caries.

MENTAL HEALTH AND ALCOHOL STUDIES

The most significant occurrence has been a steady development, extension and improvement of the State mental health program. Out-patient locations, sessions, personnel, and patients that were served have been more than doubled in the past seven years. With the State Mental Hospitals and the Department of Mental Hygiene there has been joint planning for improving at all levels the community services being provided the mentally ill. Families are trained to help discharged hospitalized patients return to community living.

Five out-patient alcohol clinics have been established in the counties and one in Baltimore City during the five years since this program has been activated. Annual scholarships have been offered to the Yale University Summer School of Alcohol Studies for a total of 63 professional people working with the alcoholic and his family.

LABORATORY SERVICES

For greater efficiency the Bacteriology and Chemistry Laboratories were merged into the Bureau of Laboratories in 1951. One of the most important functions—the control of the quality of laboratory work in the diagnosis of human disease—was extended in 1952 and further strengthened in 1957. An important addition to laboratory service has been the installation of a Virology Laboratory in 1957.

The examination of smears taken from the mouth of the uterus and certain other locations in the body enables a diagnosis of cancer to be made in early stages when treatment is effective. The Health Department in Maryland has pioneered in making this valuable preventive service available.

PUBLIC WATER SUPPLY AND SEWAGE DISPOSAL

Legislation created since 1951 has permitted local authorities to construct water or sewerage facilities with financial procedures not previously possible.

Regulations governing the subdivision of land and for the control of private water and sewerage facilities went into effect in 1953.

At the end of 1957 there were 221 public water supply and 179 sewage treatment plants in Maryland.

RADIATION HEALTH HAZARDS

Radiation is now recognized as the most dangerous instrument of our time as well as a great benefactor of mankind. Sources of exposures now include: background radiation occurring in nature, that obtained from devices such as x-ray, fluoroscopes, static eliminators, and beta gauges; commercial equipment used in radiography; radium, thorium and other normally occurring radioactive elements; some 800 synthetic or man made radioactive isotopes which are now in wide and rapidly increasing use and radioactive fall-out resulting from bomb tests. All of these sources are being watched and checked.

Clinics employing radium, x-ray, fluoroscopes, or other similar devices for therapeutic and diagnostic purposes are inspected. The Health Department follows up on all licenses for radioisotopes issued by the Atomic Energy Commission and for the past two years has cooperated with the Public Health Service in a nation-wide study on radioactive fall-out. Staff members are now receiving specialized training to prepare them for the introduction into Maryland of the next great radiation source—the nuclear power reactor.

FOOD AND DRUG CONTROL

A machine to pick the meat from crabs was constructed under the supervision of the Division of Food Control. This equipment not only eliminates 98 per cent of human contact with crab meat but is much more efficient than hand picking.

Maryland is the first State to promulgate regulations for the pasteurization of crab meat. This will enable packers to expand their markets to the midwest without danger of spoilage.

TUBERCULOSIS HOSPITALS AND CONTROL

In 1953 an additional 300 bed unit was opened at Mt. Wilson State Hospital and additional housing units were completed so that a sufficient number of personnel could live on the grounds to safeguard patients when emergencies occurred. An additional floor of 36 beds for patients was constructed at Henryton State Hospital and a new nurses home for 100 women was placed in operation. A new service wing attached to the

Victor Cullen State Hospital was placed in operation and the John Walter Smith and other antiquated buildings have been razed.

With the advent of antibiotic drugs, plus improved surgical care, approximately 60 per cent of the patients admitted each year have undergone medical rehabilitation and have been returned to the community as self-supporting citizens. Since the establishment of the surgical department at Mt. Wilson in 1956 all thoracic surgery has been performed there and the efforts of a combined surgical and medical program have shown a marked improvement in the number of patients recovering.

HOSPITAL CARE FOR THE NEEDY

The hospital in-patient program helps to finance the cost of care of low income citizens when they are acutely ill and require hospitalization. Currently 14 general hospitals in Baltimore City and 21 in the counties participate in the program. A medical review was instituted for patients remaining in the hospital beyond specified periods in order to plan earlier discharge and post-hospital care.

LICENSING HOSPITALS AND NURSING HOMES

A steady improvement has occurred in nursing home standards. Annual institutes for nursing home administrators have aided in the improvement of care.

Standards and regulations for general and special hospitals have been re-written. The Hospital Licensing Law gives the State Health Department power to revoke licenses and the 1958 law provides for imposing a fine for individual violations of the regulations.

BUILDING HOSPITALS AND HEALTH CENTERS

The hospital construction program of the Health Department is designed to assist Maryland committees in planning and financing hospitals and health centers and to disburse federal funds which are provided for constructing and improving such institutions. Thirty-two hospitals, 16 health centers, and two nursing home projects have received grants or commitments in the amount of $11,864,674 included in a total estimated construction cost of about $72,000,000. Most of the rural areas have benefited and now the larger metropolitan facilities are in line for assistance.

CHRONIC HOSPITAL PROGRAM

The old Sydenham Hospital in Baltimore, no longer needed for the care of communicable disease patients, has been converted into a chronic disease hospital and 213 beds have been added. Another addition of 180 beds together with a large area for rehabilitation services is under con-

New Administration Building, Montebello State Hospital, Baltimore.

struction. The new Western Maryland State Hospital in Hagerstown with 298 beds was opened in 1957. With Deer's Head State Hospital in Salisbury which opened in 1950 with 284 beds, the total State chronic disease hospital bed capacity is 896.

An important change in the admission policy took place with the revision of the chronic hospital law in 1957. Patients are no longer denied admission on the basis of income. Each patient and responsible members of his family are required to contribute to the cost of care.

Department of Mental Hygiene

Today our mental disease hospitals have become repositories of human trust, havens of hope.

This is a vast change from the despair and hopelessness of a recent past. That the Department of Mental Hygiene and its member hospitals have justified the public trust, is evident in rising discharge rates of patients. Public faith in the program is manifest in ready participation in hospital activities, and the thousands of hours devoted to patients' interests. The collaboration of local medical schools and national health Institutes in hospital-centered research signifies professional endorsement. Tangible evidence of improved status has been substantiated by approval of national boards of accreditation for our hospitals and for professional education.

Since 1951, there has been a 52% increase in the cost of care for each patient, but the hospitals have been able to discharge 128 more people per thousand despite almost 100 increase in admissions.

NEW BUILDINGS

Since 1951, the State has authorized the expenditure of about $18,000,000 for hospital construction to house facilities for the use of the latest remedial techniques and to care for more patients.

Although their counterparts are not yet erected in every institution, the buildings are of six main types, each with its functional purpose. Costs have been minimized by re-use of identical plans for these structures. Interiors are arranged so that a minimum of nursing personnel can take care of a maximum of patients.

Admission buildings are planned so that patients may be quickly classified, and promptly started upon active treatment schedules. Many patients return to the community without prolonged hospitalization.

Medical-surgical units are regarded as fundamental to modern psychiatric therapy, affording facilities for treatment of physical as well as mental disorders and substantially improving the prospect of recovery for patients suffering from both.

Active treatment buildings are for very sick men and women who need constant supervision and specialized psychiatric treatment. Major measures of restraint have been eliminated and long periods of seclusion curtailed.

Geriatrics units are for senior citizens with mental disorders.

Rehabilitation buildings are equipped for recreation and retraining for the return to society a whole man, an integrated personality who can carry on without extraordinary dependence on others.

Convalescent treatment cottages help expedite the transition of the patient from the hospital to the community. Here patients receive varied rehabilitative therapies including industrial training.

FOOD SERVICE

An important point indicative of improved standards of patient care is food service. Dining rooms are set up with tables for four, and patients get their meals cafeteria style on pastel plastic dishes. The food, hot, savory, planned on a basic food ration, is nutritionally adequate and carefully prepared under trained dietitians' directions. Gone are the monotonous stews of former days and the battered tin soup plates.

Basic to the accreditation granted in varying degrees to three of our hospitals is the installation of safety measures including fire doors, sprinklers and fire escapes in all of our hospitals.

For the first time, Rosewood State Training School is being developed as a center for mentally sick and handicapped children without reservation as to age or race. A positive approach to meet a need long unfilled has been effected through a residential treatment program initiated with the opening of a sixty-bed building in the spring of 1958. Here emotionally sick children under fourteen years of age for whom other community facilities were inadequate will receive dynamic treatment to restore them to their homes in relatively short periods of time.

ADULT ADMISSIONS

A long-term colony to care for adult retarded patients was opened in the summer of 1958. Eventually it will accommodate patients in residence in Rosewood and in the remaining four hospitals for the mentally ill, as well. The initial unit will provide training, continued care, and it is hoped, some rehabilitation.

A new school building contains academic classrooms, library, rooms for musical training, home economic units, training shops, gymnasium, swimming pool and an auditorium with a capacity of 900.

Nurseries for infants and crib children afford opportunity for special treatment and training during the formative years. Buildings for spastics permit children with severe neurological disorders to be grouped together for more effective medical and nursing care. Tuberculosis units secure isolation and appropriate treatment procedures.

Many adult male patients, now classified as "criminal insane," will be transferred from Spring Grove and Crownsville to a modern maximum security building in Jessups, upon its completion.

ADVANCING SERVICES

As science has advanced, we have kept pace with new medicines, improved therapies and, happily, improved results. The social service departments are stimulating procedures to prepare patients for living again in the community and are invoking the aid of community health and welfare agencies in assisting increasing numbers of convalescent patients to find niches in the world outside the hospital. Volunteers are providing resocializing experiences to help the patient adjust to the new life awaiting him.

This progress could not be recorded without the help of additional personnel. Paralleling our rising discharge rates is the rising ratio of employees to patients. The total of 2,060 employees in 1951 has risen to 3,994 in 1957.

TEACHING AND TRAINING

With a few top flight professional people to spark its program, Maryland has developed the practical device of offering courses of instruction to graduate professional personnel and to non-professional employees seeking advancement within hospital services.

Our hospitals have become teaching centers for students from Johns Hopkins and the University of Maryland medical schools. Spring Grove has been granted accreditation for approved training of psychiatric residents for three years, Springfield and Crownsville for two years, and one year respectively.

Four hospitals support approved schools for practical nursing and the fifth maintains a school for psychiatric aides. In all hospitals, attendants receive orientation courses.

Three hospitals have been designated as training centers for affiliate nurse programs in psychiatric nursing at both the diploma and university level.

A continuous training course is available to all employees desiring to become rehabilitation aides.

Four hospitals receive graduate students for training as psychology interns.

All hospitals have been accepted by various universities for field work in social services leading to a Masters degree; two hospitals for field work leading to a Doctorate degree.

PATHOLOGY

The Central Anatomic Laboratory established in 1951 has become a center of teaching, training and research in the field of neuropathology serving the State mental hospitals and several other teaching and research agencies.

RESEARCH

In recent years, there has been created a newer emphasis on the development of an atmosphere which is more conducive than ever to the pursuance of high scholarship and technical experimentation so necessary to good professional research. This has resulted in the setting up of a large number and wide variety of worthy research projects under the control of properly qualified people and with substantial and increasing financial support from State, Federal and private sources.

Such interest and support has now established professional research on a firm basis throughout the entire system of hospitals.

COMMUNITY RELATIONSHIPS

A pioneer in focusing the interest of the public in the care and treatment of the mentally ill and mentally retarded, Maryland was one of the first states to establish volunteer services under professional directors in each of its hospitals. A system of Auxiliaries initiated in 1951 has been federated into a Council which formulates policy for volunteer activities in the five hospitals, and stimulates services for the betterment of patients. Through this unique system of organizing community interest in Maryland, volunteer hours of service have risen from less than five thousand in 1951 to over ninety-six thousand in 1957.

Much remains to be learned and accomplished in the treatment of mental ills, but a growing public understanding and acceptance of the problem points the way.

We are close to the time when our construction program will be complete, and when even more attention will be given to the development of methods and medicines for more rapid cures of the afflicted, and better lives for those who cannot be cured.

The University of Maryland

Since January of 1951, the University of Maryland has experienced the most rapid growth period in its history. Developments on the campuses at College Park and at Baltimore have kept steady pace with the rising demand for opportunities in higher education.

In 1951 the total resident enrollment at College Park and at Baltimore was 10,104 students. By 1958-1959 enrollment had climbed to nearly 15,000. In the same period off-campus enrollment, both Stateside and overseas, had risen from a total of 16,737 in 1951 to 28,705 in the last fiscal year.

The record of capital improvements at College Park and at Baltimore is another impressive index of the University's progress toward becoming one of the nation's leading Land-Grant institutions.

Since 1951, the capital outlay program at College Park has placed 40 major buildings on the campus at a cost of $16,715,452. Now under construction are four dormitories, at a cost of $1,367,000. A new building for the College of Business and Public Administration at a cost of $1,550,000 will get under way within the next few months.

Since 1951, six buildings have been erected on the Baltimore campus at a cost of $4,133,099. Approximately $4,500,000 is authorized for future construction, including an allocation of $1,000,000 for the purchase of new building sites in cooperation with the Urban Renewal Agency.

This seven-year period also has been one of development in the area of public services.

EXTENSION PROGRAM

Funds for the comprehensive extension program including Fire Service Extension, and the Agricultural Extension Services of the County Agents and the Home Demonstration Agents increased from $685,745, in 1951 to $996,213 during the past fiscal year.

The University's research program including contributions from private and Federal sources has expanded from $1,159,069 in 1951 to $3,472,025 in the last fiscal year. The amount of research funds in the Physics Department alone totals in excess of $915,000 at the present time, placing the University in the front rank in the nation in the area of physics research.

New McKeldin Library at University of Maryland, College Park.

The new faculty salary scale was proposed by the Governor and approved by the Legislature in the Assembly of 1957. In effect it places the University of Maryland in a position to compete successfully for the best brains and the best talent in the market place of higher education.

The new academic probation plan, now in its first year, is a means of ensuring steady student progress toward the Bachelor Degree in a normal four or five-year period. In essence, the plan provides that a student must develop and maintain a cumulative grade point average of "C" and must obtain junior standing in 2½ years. This policy is not aimed at setting unusually high standards, but rather, at establishing a reasonable level of required performance.

LOOKING AHEAD

The University knows today that it must prepare to accept a doubled enrollment by 1970. The post-war baby-boom already is marching through the elementary levels of our educational system. Soon these students will be knocking at the doors of our colleges and universities.

In anticipation of future demands, the University of Maryland has developed a ten-year program of proposed capital outlay projects. Additionally, the Board of Regents has approved a master plan for expansion of the campus in a westerly direction to Colesville Road, creating a second axis with the new main library as a center. Engineering and science expansion will take place in a northerly direction.

The continuing aim of the University is synonymous with its present achievement: to provide excellent service to the people of the State in the areas of instruction, research and service, and to establish a pattern of leadership in all areas of educational achievement on the national scene.

Morgan State College

When Morgan State College was acquired by the State in 1939, there was a lack in every element considered basic for the conduct of a first-class college. Since that time, significant progress has been made in acquiring an adequate physical plant—a good faculty—supporting non-teaching personnel—a library, together with a varied miscellany of educational equipment. This progress is the result of a continuous increase in State financial support—both for plant and for current operations.

THE PHYSICAL PLANT

As of January, 1951, the physical plant may be briefly described as follows: 88 acres of land—a stadium—14 buildings, utilities and equipment with a total capital valuation of $4,013,887.

In 1958 the land holdings stand at 117 acres. Six obsolete buildings have been razed and ten new structures erected or are now under construction; seven buildings have undergone extensive renovation and enlargement; the capital valuation is now $8,190,146.

The campus now is improved by 22 buildings—two men's dormitories, three women's dormitories, one residence, five service buildings and 11 educational buildings; also by a stadium seating 5200, and the necessary utilities.

During this period the campus has been landscaped, tennis courts and playing fields have been laid out, parking lots constructed, campus lighting installed and a modest tree planting program completed. Capital Improvement grants amounting to $6,105,460 have provided for the expansion.

The Operating Budget for fiscal 1951 was $1,072,114
For Fiscal 1958 2,318,628

PERSONNEL

The college is operated under a nine-man Board of Trustees appointed by the Governor and confirmed by the Legislature. There is the President of the College, Dean of the College, Administrative officers, faculty and non-teaching employees.

The growth in physical facilities and student enrollment has of necessity been accompanied by an increase in personnel. It is worthy of note that the faculty now is approaching adequacy in size and composition in the light of the present enrollment; salary scales calculated to attract and hold competent teachers have been approved in successive stages. Beginning with 96 members in 1951, the instructional staff numbers 150 for 1958.

The status of the faculty is made more secure by the Teachers Retirement System—Indeterminate Tenure on earned basis—Sabbatical Leave with half pay—liberal sick and maternity leave enactments—Social Security coverage.

The number of non-teaching employees, known as the Classified Staff, has increased from 109 in 1951 to 180 in 1958. Urgently needed general salary increases were granted in 1951, 1953, 1956 and 1958. Stability is added by a policy of Internal Promotion on earned basis, the Employees Retirement System, liberal paid sick, holiday and vacation leave, Social Security coverage and adoption of the 40-hour week.

THE STUDENT BODY

Students taking regular full-time academic work in 1951 numbered 1,615. For the year 1957 the regular enrollment was 2,165, an increase of 34%.

In seven years, 1951-1957, the bachelor's degree has been earned by 1,881 graduates, an average of 270 per year.

STUDENT AID

Since many of our brightest students come from families of low income level, there is imperative need for student aid. This takes the form of a carefully administered program involving the award of scholarships and jobs, given on the basis of demonstrated need and certain minimum scholastic attainments. The largest item in this program is the grant of aid through a system of remitted fees. In 1951 aid given on the above basis amounted to $30,000. For 1958 the budgeted figure is $65,000.

SENATORIAL SCHOLARSHIPS

Each of the 29 Maryland senators is permitted to award one full scholarship to a Maryland student. During eight years 339 students have received the total sum of $112,488 from Senatorial Scholarships.

The Out-of-State Scholarship program whereby Negro students received tuition and travel expense to pursue subjects for which they were not permitted to enroll in Maryland schools has been discontinued.

CURRICULUM CHANGES AND ADMISSION REQUIREMENTS

In September, 1957, the faculty instituted a new three-level freshman curriculum. It provides three plans of study as follows:

A. Remedial help for students lacking certain basic educational skills.

B. Provision for students able to carry a normal scholastic program.

C. A program designed to challenge students of superior ability.

An entering freshman must rank in the upper three-fourths of his high school class, except that any student in the lower fourth may be admitted by examination.

A sympathetic screening and guidance program, with an expanded program of counseling, is applied to all upper classmen.

ACADEMIC RECOGNITIONS

The very signal improvement in the college educational program, particularly since the new science quadrangle was opened in 1955, has attracted gratifying attention in academic circles. Among other things

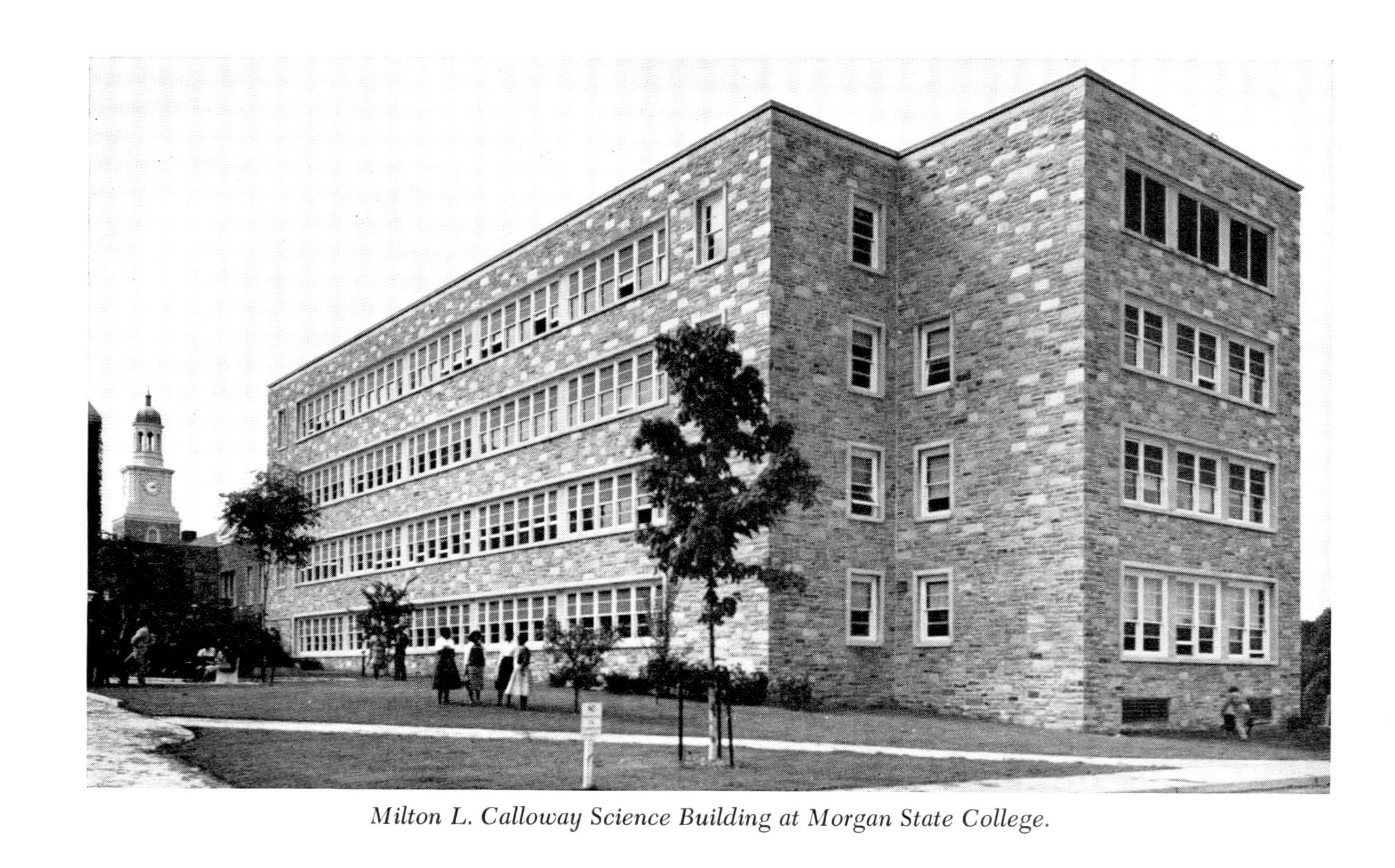

Milton L. Calloway Science Building at Morgan State College.

it has caused the federal government and other agencies to allocate several scientific projects to members of the faculty as noted below:

Physics Research:	
Department of the Army, 1953	$ 41,154
Mathematics Research:	
National Science Foundation, 1954	4,600
Chemistry Research:	
U. S. Dept. of Agriculture, 1955	10,600
National Science Foundation, 1955	13,200
The Research Corporation, 1956	3,000
Science Education:	
National Science Foundation for conduct of a summer school program for secondary School Science Teachers, 1957	66,000
1958	59,000
Fund for Advancement of Education, to finance a program to improve teaching procedures, 1957	27,000
TOTAL	$224,554

The newly strengthened department of Chemistry was approved in 1955 by the American Chemical Society.

ROTC

The Reserve Officers Training Corps basic two-year military program is required of all male students who meet prescribed standards. Upper class students who elect to do so are given the opportunity to pursue advanced work which leads to graduation and induction with officer rating into the armed services of the government. It is significant that the college, although having but a relatively small male enrollment, has maintained consistently and exceeded the federal requirement that a minimum of 25 graduate officers shall be produced each year.

The newly completed Soldiers' Armory, opened to service in September, 1957, is an extremely valuable aid to this program.

Much of the improved program and expanded facilities are too new to permit a factual report of outcomes, but progress made thus far augurs well for an increasingly successful approach to the attainment of an effective college status by Morgan State College.

Department of Education

The primary function of the State Department of Education is leadership to the local school systems. This leadership is exercised through assistance and direction in curriculum development; consultative and supervisory services to improve classroom instruction and training programs for principals, supervisors and others engaged in educational leadership responsibilities.

In 1951 the complete transition to a twelve-year school system throughout the State was accomplished, following appropriate legislation by the General Assembly of Maryland and a revision of the curriculum by a staff of local school system representatives, members of the State Department of Education and expert consultants in the different subject matter areas. In the summer of 1955 the State Department of Education in cooperation with the local school systems held a workshop at the Towson State Teachers College to restudy the curriculum and make such changes as might be deemed necessary.

After more than a year of cooperative planning, fifteen committees produced bulletins in most of the subject areas. These bulletins were reproduced and distributed to the local school systems and other educational groups within the State as well as to the State Departments of Education throughout the country. So many requests for copies of these curriculum bulletins were received from all parts of the nation that the supply soon was exhausted.

The first two of a planned series of nine conservation bulletins relating to Maryland have had several printings and still are being ordered in large quantities. A third one was published early in 1958.

VOCATIONAL REHABILITATION

In keeping with an amendment to the Social Security Act passed by Congress in 1954, Governor McKeldin designated the Division of Vocational Rehabilitation as the agency in the State to evaluate the work capacity of disabled applicants who applied to the Bureau of Old Age and Survivors' Insurance to "freeze" their social security accounts.

The Division of Vocational Rehabilitation in carrying out its responsibilities is called upon to give the benefit of its experiences in working with the disabled to reach sound and just determinations. It is expected that service will be rendered to thousands of disabled citizens as a result of an agreement with the Bureau of Old Age and Survivors' Insurance. Since January 1, 1957, the unit doing these evaluations has received an average of 400 applications per month.

TEACHER SHORTAGE

The present critical teacher shortage is an inseparable part of the larger problem—a shortage of trained manpower in all areas. Since 1950, there has been a continuing decrease in the number of college graduates. The present day college students were born during the depression period when the birth rate reached an all time low point.

We now have the anomalous situation of meeting an extremely high demand for trained manpower with the shortest supply in recent times. Competition for this small supply is becoming quite critical, especially in the teaching profession.

The public schools in Maryland need approximately 3,600 new teachers each year. The total combined output of all colleges and universities in the State is approximately 1,000 teachers per year, thus leaving a deficiency of 2,600. To meet this need, the staff of the State Department of Education and the local school authorities have engaged in an intensive recruitment program for the past five years.

TEACHERS' SALARIES

The average salary for a public school teacher in Maryland was $3,543 in 1950-51. It had increased to $4,604 in 1956-57. This marked increase in teachers' salaries has been due to increased State financial assistance through a new State minimum salary scale which was enacted in 1953 and to the efforts of the local school systems to provide financial support for salary scales in excess of the guaranteed minimum by the State. In 1952 Governor McKeldin appointed a commission to study the problem of a proposed new State minimum salary scale.

This Commission recommended a provision for a new minimum salary scale.

During the two-year period from 1953-54 to 1954-55, a transition scale of $2,500 to $4,300 was in effect. Those local political subdivisions paying less than this scale at the time of the passage of the law received State aid to enable them to pay the transitional scale. Beginning September, 1956, a new permament State minimum salary scale of $2,800 to $4,600 became effective.

The minimum salary law enacted in 1958 increased the guaranteed State minimum scale by $400, making the minimum scale for 1958-59 $3,200-$5,000.

Generally, these basic State-prescribed minimums are substantially supplemented by City and County funds.

SCHOOL BUILDING CONSTRUCTION

Since 1950, there has been expended approximately $280,000,000 for the construction of public school buildings in the State. Most of this amount has been spent for new construction and only a relatively small part for the alteration and remodeling of existing buildings. Each year approximately 900 classrooms have been built. This construction has provided an increased pupil capacity of approximately 170,000.

Funds for constructing these new buildings have come primarily from local tax sources. However, the State has been making an increasingly larger contribution toward school construction since 1947, when the first school building Incentive Fund was established by law. Beginning in 1947 and up to 1956, the State was contributing approximately $1,125,000 annually through the school building Incentive Fund for school building construction.

In 1956 the law was revised to provide an additional $10 per pupil from this fund, thus increasing the annual contribution from the State by $5,000,000. In 1949 the State made available a flat grant of $20,000,000 for school building construction, on a one-to-three matching basis.

TEACHERS COLLEGES

During the past seven years there has been a sharp increase in enrollments at the State teachers colleges with a consequent need for additional physical facilities. The State has appropriated $6,390,000 for buildings which already have been constructed or are in the planning stage.

Salaries for the faculty members at the colleges have been increased substantially since 1951. The maximum scale for an instructor with a master's degree has been increased $1,700 while the maximum for the doctorate has been increased $2,200. In addition, a new category "master's plus 30" has been established with a scale approximately midway between the master's and doctorate scales.

The State teachers colleges are maintained by the State to prepare young people for State service in the profession of teaching. There is no tuition charge and the young people sign a pledge to teach at least two years in the State. Each year more than 90 per cent of the graduates become teachers within the State. This is far in excess of the experience for other States operating comparable teachers colleges.

Public Junior Colleges

The Eisenhower Commission on Higher Education has stated that by 1970 the enrollments in our colleges and universities will be more than doubled. The Commission appointed by the Governor to study this and related problems concerning higher education reached a unanimous conclusion that existing institutions of higher education in Maryland would be unable to take care of this great influx.

The Commission unanimously recommended the establishment of a system of public junior colleges throughout the State operated by the local school systems to provide courses of a terminal nature and the usual freshmen and sophomore courses which would be offered in a four-year institution. Young people, in line with the nationwide trend, can live at home and go to college nearby without too great an expense.

This system of public junior colleges has been planned to meet the needs of all potential students regardless of geographical location. To date seven of these new institutions are in operation at the following locations: Baltimore City, Takoma Park, Hagerstown, Frederick, Bel Air, Catonsville and Essex.

Desegregation in the Public Schools

Following the opinion of the Supreme Court of the United States on May 17, 1954, that all State laws and regulations which required or permitted racial discrimination in public education are unconstitutional, the State Board of Education, on May 26, 1954, passed unanimously a declaration of intention.

The following three paragraphs from the statement might be considered the highlights:

"The Supreme Court of the land has spoken. It is the duty and responsibility of the State Board of Education to do all within its power to work out the problem seemingly and in order and in such manner that the rights and privileges of no individual are impaired by arbitrary and capricious methods.

"The laws of Maryland specifically provide for segregation in the public schools and in the teachers colleges. In view of this law requiring segregation, no program of integration can be put into effect until the decision of the Supreme Court becomes final and an effective date is set by the Supreme Court.

"The role of the State Board of Education is not to set the detailed pattern of operation but to take an official position that the decision will be implemented with fairness and justice to all, and with due regard for the professional aspects of the program. Further, its responsibility is to act in a general over-all supervisory nature to insure that standard, equitable practices are followed throughout the State."

All the local political subdivisions took immediate action to desegregate the public schools. Baltimore City began to desegregate its schools during the school year 1954-55. The County school systems appointed local citizens' committees to study the problem and make recommendations to the boards of education. At present all the school systems of the State have taken some positive action to desegregate the public schools.

School for the Deaf

The Maryland School for the Deaf is a free public residential school, which has been serving the educational needs of Maryland children with impaired hearing since its founding in 1868.

Progress since that time has been one of steady growth in terms of enrollment, personnel and buildings. The period from 1951 to the present has seen increased responsibilities that have brought about some of the most rapid changes and improvements ever experienced in the history of the school.

Funds for a new Library were provided in the amount of $190,000. The Library was designed to provide modern library facilities, study areas for boys and girls, a conference room and a sound-treated area for testing children. Since the completion of this building in 1953, its function has been a tremendous factor in the academic progress of the school.

In 1953, $225,000 were provided for the construction of a new plant for heating and laundry facilities. The new heating plant provides the school with the most modern equipment of its type to serve five buildings with heat and hot water. Final costs totaled $252,564 when the heating plant and laundry facilities were put into operation in 1954.

With $22,000 approved by the General Assembly of 1956 and

$8,100 provided by the Board of Visitors, a new residence for the Superintendent was erected in 1957-58.

INCREASED APPROPRIATIONS

Increased responsibilities and services have been reflected in the annual appropriations of $196,378 in 1951, $255,034 in 1955 and $330,808 in 1957. Increased appropriations enabled the Maryland School for the Deaf to raise the number of personnel from 62 to 75 during this period, including teachers, houseparents and engineering and maintenance staff. Salaries of employees and teachers have been increased enabling the school to retain its reputation for small turnovers in personnel.

At all times the major emphasis of the school is continuous improvement in academic, vocational, social and recreational programming. Since 1945, and particularly since 1950, there has been a vast improvement in electronic amplification for the purpose of helping students who may benefit from amplified sound to hear, and in turn, improve their speech and lipreading skills.

To date, ten classrooms are equipped with the finest auditory training equipment available, consisting of special amplifiers, microphones and ten headphones to each room. As a result of this equipment, more children have found individual wearable hearing aids of greater benefit, as shown by the large number of children using such aids each day in all the instructional, recreational and social activities of the school.

At the present time 50 per cent of the hearing-impaired children wear individual hearing aids out of 166 children enrolled in the school. Starting in 1958, a teacher will devote full time to supervising the testing of hearing, the use of individual wearable hearing aids and the auditory training program and to teaching speech and lipreading on a tutoring basis and in group work.

NEW EVALUATION PROGRAM

In 1956 a new program of evaluation and differential screening of applicants was instituted, including the taking of case histories and the evaluating of social maturity, language and speech skills, intelligence and hearing. Through the new screening and evaluation program, the problems of each child are more clearly understood and appreciated.

Vocationally, the program has been expanded sharply with the construction of an Industrial Arts Department in the Vocational Building. In addition to cabinet making and printing, the school can offer a wide variety of learning experiences in the Industrial Arts program.

The latter offers learning opportunities in ceramics, plastics, leather, art and sheet metal and basic woodworking. Various power tools peculiar to these areas, hand tools and power machinery give the boys the wide variety of training and skills necessary for eventual placement in industry in the State of Maryland.

In 1957 the Arts and Crafts Department was given new emphasis with the construction of two spacious and well-lighted rooms in the basement of the Academic Building.

COOPERATIVE AGREEMENT

In 1957 a cooperative working argreement and relationship between the Maryland School for the Deaf, the State Board and State Department of Education was established.

The office of Vocational Rehabilitation furnishes the services of a counselor who serves the school in vocational testing and counseling of all students over 15 years of age and in vocational placement of graduates. In effect, this service completes a wide range program in which the school educates the deaf and the hard-of-hearing from kindergarten through high school, sending qualified students to Gallaudet College in Washington, D. C., and providing proper placement in various industries in Maryland.

Seminars have been held at the school for Vocational Rehabilitation Counselors and Speech Therapists from the public schools and for Audiologists from the Hearing and Speech Centers of Gallaudet College and the Johns Hopkins Hospital.

Leaders in the profession of audiology and language problems conducted three-day workshops at the school in 1956 and 1957. As a result of these two workshops, the teachers have increased their knowledge and achieved better understanding and appreciation of the deaf. Opportunities were enhanced for effective application of this knowledge to improve instruction, and teachers received extremely vital professional stimulation.

ENROLLMENT GROWTH

Growth in enrollment is shown by an increase from 136 in 1951 to 166 in 1958. To meet the problem of growth, the Board of Visitors appointed a Ten Year Capital Improvements Committee, consisting of members of the Board, representatives from the State Departments of Health and Education, consultants from the State Planning Commission and from the State Department of Public Improvements, the President of Gallaudet College and the Superintendent of the West Virginia School for the Deaf. As a result of its initial work, progress toward a building program has been made by the inclusion of $10,000 in the Capital Improvements recommendations for architectural and planning fees for a

Primary Building to house, feed and educate deaf and hard-of-hearing children between the age of five and 11 years.

This will enable the school to teach and to manage more effectively the entire program of instruction, residential living and recreational programs.

The enrollment of the school shows increases will come in future years. The Ten Year Capital Improvements Committee recommendations are planned to meet these needs.

State Teachers College at Towson

ENROLLMENT

The total enrollment in 1951-1952 was 880. The enrollment in September, 1957, was 1256—approximately a 50 per cent increase. For the past several years, the enrollment has gone up about 100 students each year. This year the enrollment did not increase but, with high school classes growing larger, the enrollment for the 1958 semester is expected to show another increase. The enrollment includes about 950 women and 300 men. Of the total enrollment, slightly fewer than 100 are enrolled in the junior college program, over 1100 being in the Teachers College.

In 1951 there were 144 graduates. The number in June, 1958, was 249. Although the increase in the number of graduates is gratifying, it still comes far short of meeting the needs of the school systems we serve. Either Baltimore City or Baltimore County or any one of several of the larger Counties could absorb our entire graduating class.

It is gratifying to report also that the quality of students remains high. Each Fall we administer a set of national tests to freshmen and can compare our results with those in two or three hundred other colleges throughout the country. For the last several years our freshman scores have been above the national average.

PROGRAM

The college has continued to offer preparation for teaching in three divisions—kindergarten-primary, elementary and junior high. In addition, we have had since 1946 a small group of junior college students—many of whom transfer to the Teachers College program at the end of two years.

After considerable study by the presidents and faculties of the five

Teachers Colleges, new curriculum requirements were proposed to the State Board of Education. These were approved in the summer of 1953. The new requirements give more opportunity for student selection while continuing to place emphasis on a broad program of general education and an adequate program of professional education. Roughly one-half of the required four-year course is in specified areas of English, history, science, mathematics, art, music, physical education and psychology. Approximately one-quarter is taken up with professional courses, including student teaching. The remainder of the program is open for student election from either the professional or the general field.

The summer program, which began in 1949, has continued to grow. In 1951, 148 students were enrolled and in 1958 the number had grown to 687. The summer program for 1958 was organized in three divisions: (1) professional courses for graduates of liberal arts colleges who wish to prepare for elementary teaching; (2) undergraduate courses for teachers in the field who have not yet received their degree, and for Teachers College students who need, or wish, to take summer courses; (3) graduate courses leading to the Master of Education Degree for elementary teachers.

Also, for the past several years, the college has operated a number of "late afternoon classes" which are open to teachers of nearby schools who need to take additional work in order to complete their Bachelor's Degrees. Many of these teachers are among those who also take advantage of the summer program.

The college has had the advantage of being reviewed for accreditation by several agencies during recent years. Approval was first given by the Middle States Association of Colleges and Schools in 1949, and the college will be reviewed by this Association again in 1959. The president of the college has been a member of the Commission on Higher Institutions and of the Executive Committee of the Middle States Association for the past seven years. In 1952 the college made request to be approved by the American Association of University Women and received approval—the fifth college in the State thus to be recognized.

In 1953 the American Association of Colleges for Teacher Education sent a committee to study the college program, and its report has been of value in the development of the college. In its summary, the committee said, "In general, the committee believes that this is a strong institution with a forward-looking administrative procedure."

The various student organizations on campus, under the leadership of the Student Government Association, have issued a "Student Leadership Manual" and for the past several years have operated a week-end Student Leadership Work Shop at a nearby camp.

PHYSICAL FACILITIES

A great many physical changes have been made on the campus since 1951. The Bond Issue of 1949 appropriated more than one million dollars for new facilities—the largest single appropriation in the institution's 92 years of existence. None of the facilities provided in this appropriation, however, was available until 1951. In that year the two Men's Residence Halls, accommodating more than 100 students, were dedicated and occupied, and a new tile-drained athletic field was constructed on the western part of the campus.

In 1952 a new high power boiler was installed; 1953 saw the opening of the remodeled dining hall, new kitchen unit and new Student Centre, the latter being made possible through remodeling of the former kitchen area. In 1954, an appropriation of more than one-half million dollars was provided for the much needed new library building, and in 1956 a similar appropriation was made for an additional women's residence hall. Both of these buildings were opened in the Fall, 1957, and have added a great deal to the effectiveness of the college program.

In 1954, through the cooperation of the Department of Public Improvements, a firm of experts was engaged to assist in a comprehensive long-term campus plan, and all new buildings are being located in line with their recommendations. Two appropriations—1955, and 1956—were for acquiring additional land. One small plot north of the campus has been obtained and negotiations are being completed with the Sheppard-Pratt Hospital authorities for about 25 additional acres adjoining the present campus on the west. This will bring the total campus size to nearly 100 acres.

The Bond Issue of 1957 provided funds for a new campus laboratory school, which will be under construction in the near future. When this building is completed, the present laboratory school will be remodeled to provide additional college classroom space—the first addition to the academic classroom facilities since 1915. Also, the moving of the library to its new quarters made some available space in the main building, and this has been remodeled for administrative offices and classroom space.

Other appropriations during recent years have provided for rebuilding the campus lighting system and resurfacing campus roads, modernizing the lighting of all academic classrooms, rebuilding the tower clock, renewing stage curtains and modernizing the stage lighting system in the auditorium, replacing broken terra cotta tile on the two oldest buildings and adding some much needed parking lots to the campus.

On the lower floor of the main building, a Branch Post Office, installed in 1956, is operated through a contract with the Baltimore Post

Office. A small chapel was built adjacent to the Student Centre, partly through the contributions of student help and student funds, and an outdoor patio was added to the facilities of the Student Centre.

All in all, the campus has had many additions and much "face lifting" during the past several years. More will be needed, of course, if enrollment continues to grow—which seems almost a certainty.

MISCELLANEOUS

Under the leadership of the Admissions Office, a concentrated "recruitment program" has been developed to interest high school students in the field of teaching as a career. Visits are made annually to every high school in our geographical area, and a series of "high school visiting days" was organized to bring high school students to the campus.

Through the English department, a new literary magazine, called "Towers," was started five years ago to provide students with creative art and writing ability an outlet for their talent.

The orienation program for freshmen has been expanded in recent years under the direction of a carefully selected group of freshmen advisors. Following the usual Freshman Orientation Week, the freshmen meet their advisors regularly once a week for instruction in adjusting to college life and study and an introduction to the various phases of public education.

An "Administrative Manual" for the benefit of administrators and faculty has been developed and revised periodically. It includes a listing of the responsibilities and duties of all administrators and a description of committee functions.

Through a bequest left the Alumni Association, as well as contributions of various alumni, a part-time alumni secretary has been employed.

This Spring, a new idea in public relations was begun with the inaugurating of an "Open House" for friends and neighbors of the community. One afternoon and evening all buildings were open, student guides were available and approximately 1,000 persons visited the campus.

For the last several years, the college has profited from the advice and suggestions received from a "Consulting Committee" which meets on the campus once or twice a year. The committee is composed of representatives from the school systems of Baltimore City, Baltimore County, all the neighboring school systems and the State Department of Education.

Bowie State Teachers College

The growth of the Bowie State Teachers College during the past seven years has outdistanced that of the combined years of prior existence. Major accomplishments are apparent in the areas of capital improvement, upgrading of personnel, curriculum revision and expansion, library services, professional experiences and in the improved caliber of graduates.

CAPITAL IMPROVEMENTS

Exactly ten years after moving to its present site, the institution received $18,000 for the construction of a residence hall for women students. There was no further expansion of the physical plant until 1924 when $100,000 was provided for the construction of a new administration building and men's dormitory. These are typical appropriations prior to 1951.

By comparison, since 1951, there has been an expenditure of approximately $1,250,000 for new buildings and equipment. These include a library, gymnasium, auditorium, a women's residence hall and other improvements.

FACULTY AND STAFF PERSONNEL

Larger appropriations have made possible an increase in the instructional staff from 15 in 1951 to 18 in 1957. Similarly, the administrative officers and staff have grown from 15 in 1951 to 20 in 1957.

Many of the present positions now essential in the administration of educating our students were not operative seven years ago. Such provision is bringing the college within the range of the expectations of national accrediting agencies.

When the college attained the ability to hire more and better qualified instructors, the teaching load reached a normal level and greater enrichment became possible through course offerings and in instruction.

Course offerings have been augmented by a State policy which has permitted the inclusion of as many as 28 semester hours of electives in the total requirements for graduation. This provision makes it possible for the college to offer students a wider choice in relation to needs and, consequently, additional opportunities for growth in the area of general education. Such a program is helping the college to produce better prepared teachers for our public schools.

Since the college is rurally located, and since the majority of the students come from rural communities in the State, the allocation in the budget for a cultural arts program has enabled the college to broaden and deepen the cultural background of the group through media heretofore unavailable to them.

For years Bowie was unable to offer an adequate extracurricular program usually associated with college life. But, with the development of the physical plant and especially the completion of the McKeldin Gymnasium, it now is possible to provide a stronger intramural program, functional dramatics and other socializing activities which contribute so much to the development of those competencies desired in those who will teach.

Since the college is concerned not only with the development of those attitudes, habits, skills, knowledge and appreciations that will insure teaching efficiency, but also with the development of these same attributes to insure community betterment and the perpetuation of democracy, a practice cottage was made a part of the program in 1951. Our graduates make use of what they have learned in the cottage; the fact is evidenced in the ever-growing percentage of home ownership among graduates and participation in projects and organizations designed to improve family life in rural Maryland.

LIBRARY

More than 7,500 volumes have been added to the library since 1951. Seven years ago there were only a few bound periodicals in the collection; at present there are 503. The audio-visual aids equipment has been expanded from one projector to several machines, filmstrips and recordings. The library now subscribes to 287 periodicals as contrasted to 150 in 1951.

Work crews are preparing the foundation for Bowie's new library, scheduled for completion by September, 1959. It will have ample space to house more than 60,000 volumes.

PROFESSIONAL EXPERIENCES

Prior to 1951, approximately 15 student teaching situations were available, necessitating the placing of several students in a single room for this serious training. In contrast, there are now 80 rooms at the college's disposal. This increase is the result of additional appropriations, and makes possible the placing of one cadet teacher to a room.

Since many of the teachers of the State are graduates of this college and more than 80% of them have achieved tenure, and are, therefore, stable in their positions, it would seem that the increased investment is merited.

The investment also has a human interest aspect when we view with satisfaction the large number of graduates who have matriculated at the leading universities of the East, and have earned advanced degrees.

Coppin State Teachers College

This institution was transferred from control of Baltimore City to the State of Maryland in 1950. Since that time, there has been a gradual increase in enrollment, faculty and staff members; in library facilities; in curriculum offerings; in operational budget; and in certain appropriations for capital improvement.

The enrollment of this institution has expanded from 199 students in 1950-51 to 333 students in 1957-58. This increase in enrollment has necessitated an increase in faculty and staff from nine faculty and two staff members in 1950-51 to 18 faculty and 21 staff members in 1957-58.

The total number of graduates of this institution between the years 1950-51 and 1956-57 was 352, an average of slightly more than 50 graduates per year. More than 95 per cent of these graduates accepted teaching positions in the Baltimore City Schools.

During the period 1950-58, the library staff has increased from one full-time librarian in 1950-51 to one full-time librarian, one assistant librarian, one library assistant and one junior typist. During this eight-year period, the library has acquired 8,510 volumes at a cost of $28,023. The library currently is processing approximately 3,000 volumes, which will bring the total number of volumes to around 11,510.

In July, 1951, an appropriation of $635,000 was made for the purchase and improvement of the present site of Coppin State Teachers College. Subsequent to the purchase of the site, $935,000 has been appropriated, making a total appropriation of $1,670,500 for capital improvement. There have been total appropriations amounting to $1,152,365 for operation of the institution for the period 1952 through 1958.

Our professional program has expanded from a single curriculum in general elementary education in 1950-51 to a dual curriculum, which includes general elementary teacher training and kindergarten-primary teacher training. The kindergarten-primary progam was initiated in September, 1955.

Students leaving main building at Coppin State Teachers College

Salisbury State Teachers College

The seven years covered by this report were most significant years for the State Teachers College in Salisbury. Not only was the College able to expand its physical facilities, but also to improve and refine greatly its curricular offerings, to increase the professional and non-professional personnel and to enrich student life.

The Capital Improvement Program at the College has been characterized by a systematic and well-organized plan of development. The College campus of thirty acres and one main building has been enlarged, by the purchase of land and construction of new buildings, to a campus of sixty-two acres and four buildings. In the Fall of 1951 a men's dormitory, accommodating one hundred men, was completed and occupied for the first time. In the Fall of 1955 a new Campus Elementary School was completed, thereby improving greatly the teacher education program of the College. In the Fall of 1957 a new library building, modern in every respect, was occupied, bringing to the college program a much needed academic resource, and making it possible for the instructional program of the College to be enriched greatly.

Also in the Fall of 1957 the science department was moved into a wing of the main building which was used formerly as the Campus Elementary School. This wing was completely remodeled and now houses an up-to-date and well-equipped set of laboratories, lecture room and faculty offices. The space in the main building formerly occupied by the library is being converted at the present time into a student center, thereby providing much needed facilities for student organizations and recreational activities.

Aside from this major construction, changes have been made in original plant facilities which increase their use and effect economy in maintenance.

NEW AUDITORIUM

At the present time an auditorium is being added to the Campus Elementary School. Upon completion of this facility the College will have a complete Campus Elementary School with all resources needed for carrying on a good program of education, not only for the pupils enrolled in that School, but for the student teachers and all other students enrolled in the college program. It is the Campus Elementary School that serves as the laboratory for many of the college courses, both in general and professional education.

During these seven years a total of $1,481,679 has been made available for the general physical development of the College.

During this same period of time the curriculum has undergone careful scrutiny and revision to the end that the program offers to all students not only a good basic general education, but also a well-balanced program for developing professional skills needed in the teaching process.

Through the addition of several courses in history, geography and science, a much more comprehensive program now is available to all students.

The Library is the most important service center in the instructional program of the College. As the curriculum expands in breadth and depth, additional resources are needed to enrich and vitalize the instruction. In 1951 there were 21,931 volumes in the College Library and 400 volumes in the Campus Elementary School Library; in 1958 there are 28,739 volumes in the College Library and 3,898 volumes in the Campus Elementary School Library.

INCREASED ENROLLMENT

The trend in the enrollment during these seven years is significant. In 1950-51 the total enrollment of the College was 223. Of this number 123 or 55.2 per cent were enrolled in teacher education, and 100 or 44.8 per cent were enrolled in the transfer program. In 1957-58 the total enrollment is 328, or a gain in these seven years of 105 students. Of the 328 enrolled, 267 or 81 per cent are enrolled in the teacher education curriculum, and only 61 or 19 per cent in the transfer program. These figures indicate the gain that we have been able to make in the number of students who are preparing to teach in our public schools.

As the enrollment increased, the physical facilities have been expanded and improved, and additional personnel, both professional and classified, has been added to service the program. The 1950-51 budget provided for 26 professional and 29 classified employees. The 1957-58 budget provides for 32 professional and 50 classified employees. Of the 32 professional employees, 12 or 37 per cent held the doctor's degree, and ten or 30 per cent the master's degree, plus 30 additional graduate hours. This means that 22 or approximately 70 per cent of the instructional staff has completed graduate work in excess of the master's degree.

Thus we see that progress has been made toward keeping the staff, both professional and classified, in line with the growth in enrollment, the improvement in curricular program and the development of the physical facilities.

The accreditation of an institution of higher education is most important. The State Teachers College at Salisbury prior to 1956 was accredited by the American Association of Colleges for Teacher Education, as well as by the Maryland State Board of Education. In 1956 the College was visited by the Middle States Association of Colleges and Secondary Schools, and as a result of that visit the College received accreditation by that group. This represents one of the most significant achievements in the history of the College. It means that the State Teachers College at Salisbury now is fully accredited by State, regional and national agencies.

Frostburg State Teachers College

Prior to 1951 Frostburg State Teachers College campus consisted of Frost Hall, Old Main, Cold Hall and Allegany Hall.

By the beginning of the 1950-51 academic year the campus included additional properties purchased for expansion purposes, so that the campus then represented about forty acres valued at $1,000,000.

The new $240,173 Garrett Hall was constructed to replace the wartime temporary building and to provide additional space needed for instruction of students in the sciences. This building, completed early in 1952, includes four laboratories, a dark room, two classrooms, four offices for the science instructors, storage, and cloakroom facilities.

In 1954, Lowndes Hall, a library and administration building, costing—with equipment and utilities—$399,600, was completed. This structure provided modern and adequate library facilities on the first floor and administrative offices on the second floor.

Compton Hall was completed in 1955 at a cost of $701,613, including equipment. This building houses health and physical education classes, music, modern languages and an auditorium for assemblies, including lectures and theatrical productions.

Completed in 1956 were Allen Hall and Simpson Hall, valued at $569,505. These two residence halls alleviated overcrowded conditions in Frost Hall and also provided for the first time the opportunity for men students to live on campus.

During the past seven-year period, an additional $315,600 was spent on improvements of the physical plant and grounds of the College.

In 1956, the State provided $350,000 for a dining hall and student activities building with $72,000 to equip this structure. Bids have twice exceeded the appropriation, but when this building is constructed, it will replace a presently outmoded dining hall. Seven thousand dollars also was made available for plans for a Laboratory School.

The 1957 Assembly appropriated $610,000 for the construction of this Laboratory School, $45,000 for site improvements and $64,000 for expansion and relocation of athletic facilities.

Expansion of the physical plant has resulted from an increasing enrollment and a developing educational program. When the State Normal School at Frostburg opened in 1902, fifty-seven students enrolled. In 1931 the professional course of study was increased to three years by an act of the General Assembly. In 1934 the course for elementary teachers was increased to four years, and the granting of the degree of Bachelor of Science was authorized. In 1947 the program for preparation of junior high school teachers was introduced. By 1955 the college reached a maximum capacity of 629 students in all areas of study.

The total approximate value of the campus, when all the above work is completed, will be $4,470,000.

Maryland Commission on Interracial Problems and Relations

In the interpretation of the activities of the Maryland Commission on Interracial Problems and Relations, it is necessary to point out the responsibilities of this Commission.

> "The said Commission shall have authority and power to make such surveys and studies concerning interracial relations, conditions and problems as it may determine to promote in every way possible the welfare of the colored race and the betterment of interracial relations."

Segregation of races in Ford's Theater was lifted by agreement of the management of Ford's Theater and the Commission, effective Friday, February 1, 1952.

The consideration of executives of various department stores to eliminate gradually racial discriminations in their respective department stores began during the year 1952.

Following the issuance of the report of the Baltimore Transit Commission recommending that the Transit Company amend its personnel policies to permit the employment of Negro bus and trolley operators, the Commission urged the Transit Company to put the recommendation into effect at the earliest possible date. Between May and November, 1952, the Transit Company employed 180 Negroes.

With the full support of the Governor, this Commission presented a resolution to the Baltimore Board of School Commissioners on September 2, 1952 advocating the admission of Negro applicants to the "A" course at Baltimore Polytechnic Institute. Fifteen Negro applicants subsequently were admitted, and the policy of integration continued, well in advance of the Supreme Court anti-segregation decision.

Through the efforts of a sub-committee of the Maryland Interracial Commission, by agreement with the board of the Lyric Theater, on November 12, 1953, the Lyric ended certain policies which were considered deleterious to good race relations.

August 1, 1953 marked the start of the Community Self-Survey project. This survey was a comprehensive study of intergroup relations in the City of Baltimore directing its major attention toward conditions affecting the minority population, with particular emphasis upon the Negro. This study was co-sponsored by the Baltimore Commission on Human Relations and 65 civic, fraternal, religious and private agencies. The Community Self-Survey was completed early in 1955 and represented the first such study undertaken and completed by a southern city.

Another important advance in 1953 was the opening of lunch counter service to Negroes by two large chain variety stores as a result of negotiations carried on mainly by the Congress of Racial Equality in cooperation with the efforts of the Maryland Commission.

During the year 1954, largely through the efforts of this Commission, integration was begun in the Baltimore City Fire Department.

In 1955 the following achievements were effected: a large drugstore chain adopted a policy ending racial discrimination in hiring personnel; the State of Maryland began employing Negro toll-takers on the Susquehanna and Chesapeake Bay bridges and the banning of racial segregation of State-owned beaches and parks.

A study entitled "Desegregation in the Baltimore City Schools" was completed in 1956. This study provided a definitive analysis of the process of desegregation in the Baltimore City schools. It has been used as a pattern by many communities throughout the country in the promulgation of the desegregation process. It has had international circulation and is one of the three best studies in this area of desegregation in the nation. The Commission's activities through its survey helped pave the way for desegregation in the Baltimore Schools.

The Commission is able to conclude this report in saying that most of the major hotels in Baltimore City now provide accommodations for all peoples.

Department of Correction

In the past eight years marked development has taken place in the Department of Correction of the State of Maryland. This growth has included not only the expansion of facilities to keep pace with the growing prison population but also the adoption of the best of approved new methods and techniques in the field of correction.

In a concerted effort to improve our system, all existing institutions have been expanded and modernized in the course of the years. Physically, this has meant new buildings, renovation of older structures and the demolition of those unfit for use. It further entailed modernization of heating, lighting and power systems and the replacing of such equipment as kitchen and laundry installations.

The period was marked by an extension of the system of prisoner employment under the State Use Industries, general expansion of academic and vocational education, and the institution of full-time Chaplains.

By far the most significant development was the opening of Patuxent Institution for Defective Delinquents, where the full force of modern psychiatric progress is being brought to the assistance of the Department of Correction. This institution, all but unique in character, with the only similar one being at Herstedvester, Denmark, is a major forward step in correction work. Time will prove the full extent of its effectiveness. In this Institution will be a diagnostic center, funds for which have been appropriated and for which plans are now in progress. Upon its completion, it will serve as a diagnostic center for all the Courts of Maryland, as well as for all institutions under the Department of Correction.

PATUXENT INSTITUTION

The Patuxent Institution for Defective Delinquents was established by Act of Legislature in 1951 and received its first inmates on January 4, 1955. To date the Institution has been concentrating its efforts in the areas of personnel work, inmate management, diagnosis, treatment and research.

A testing program was initiated to secure stable, well oriented personnel and extended later to the entire Department. This work on testing is closely tied with the Commissioner of Personnel's office and may result in a satisfactory written testing procedure for statewide selection of custodial officers. The Institution also initiated a continuous In-Service Training program for the education of custodial personnel in relation to custodial work and management of problems posed by the special population of the Institution.

Since the Institution is in the unique position of being under psychiatric direction, the diagnostic and treatment programs are of prime importance, and are psychiatrically oriented. The inmate is encouraged to set realistic goals toward which to work.

The Institution is required by the courts to perform diagnostic evaluation and give treatment, when appropriate, for those committed. Its function is not only to detect sociopathic persons but to prevent them from committing crimes, and also to treat them with a view to their return to the community as productive citizens if and when they are no longer dangerous to the social body.

This area is the greatest challenge and opportunity for the Institution. With the cooperation of leading drug companies, drug research is starting on the treatment of defective delinquents with major emphasis on the sex offender. There is also a program of drug research and treatment to investigate the somatic relationship of stress and anxiety-producing situations in relation to emotional content and character structure. Studies are being made in the field of the electroencephalogram and a major report is expected within the year. It is expected that this work will shed light on the physiological factors in the sociopathic personality.

Further research involving conditioning techniques is under way and has reached the pre-publication stage. The Institution also cooperated with the National Institute of Mental Health in Geriatric Research and in testing Asiatic Flu Vaccine.

At Patuxent Institution, since its opening in 1955, efforts have been made to establish, on a progressively advancing basis, a well integrated and balanced research and therapeutic program incorporating the use of drugs, group therapy, occupational therapy and milieu therapy.

The aim of this program is to attempt to salvage and rehabilitate, to the maximum extent possible, the defective delinquent.

MARYLAND PENITENTIARY

In this institution the major accomplishment has been the erection of a new 60-bed general hospital which ranks with the most modern in the country. This hospital not only cares for inmates of the Penitentiary, but is further intended to provide medical, surgical and clinical services for all male institutions under the jurisdiction of the Department of Correction.

Miscellaneous improvements include demolition of useless buildings dating from 1811; erection of a new death house and lethal gas chamber; changes in lighting and heating; relocation of industrial shops and the addition of new ones to the industries program.

The educational system has reached the point where 650 inmates attend courses ranging from elementary and vocational education to a Freshman College course given in conjunction with the University of Maryland.

The services of a full-time Chaplain since 1957 have made the religious life of the institution more general and much more effective in improving the morals and morale of the inmates.

Prisoners transferred from the Penitentiary to Poplar Hill Correctional Camp located in Wicomico County, farm a 241-acre tract of land and are producing crops used as a food supply for the correctional institutions and canneries of the Department.

HOUSE OF CORRECTION

This institution has felt the growth of population during the past eight years in a marked degree. To accommodate the increased numbers, a new dormitory wing was erected to care for an additional 450 inmates. Two warehouses with 28,000 square feet of space have been erected to meet this need.

Numerous smaller buildings have been erected as need has arisen from year to year. In addition, vital improvements have been made in existing plant and equipment, including a new storage dam to insure adequate water supply for the institution.

The program of the States Use Industries has been enlarged at the institution and the older shops modernized by the replacement of older equipment.

Full-time Chaplain services are also a major recent accomplishment.

A correctional Camp established in 1955 in Charles County and known as the Southern Maryland Correctional Camp, was started for the purpose of transferring inmates from the House of Correction to be assigned to work projects of the State Roads Commission and the County Commissioners of the several Southern Maryland Counties.

REFORMATORY FOR WOMEN

This institution has shown steady growth in the years since 1951. As with all correctional institutions in the State, it has felt the need of additional living units and has met this need with the erection of Lane Cottage, caring for 50 additional inmates.

Improvement in the services at the institution was more important than mere increase in size. The opening of a new State Use Industries

Building in 1952 made possible an increase in the employment of prisoners, and also, through the establishment of a canning unit, assured the saving of many crop surpluses from the adjacent farm.

Of great importance has been the enlargement of the educational system and particularly work done to enable inmates to secure High School Equivalence Certificates as a result of examinations taken from the Department of Education.

Cultural and social advances have gone far beyond mere classroom activity. Religious life and activity has been made more vital through increased Chaplain facilities. Rehabilitative work is also improving as evidenced by a flourishing Alcoholics Anonymous group and a new but developing Narcotics Anonymous unit called the Renaissance Group.

REFORMATORY FOR MALES

This institution notes in its record for the past eight years a major accomplishment in the field of new construction. Much work has been done employing prison labor exclusively. Among the many masonry block buildings erected were a cannery building housing equipment that is now preparing foods for use in agencies throughout the State; a feed mixing mill for the preparation of animal and poultry feed; a shop building to house the woodworking operation; a garage to house automotive equipment as well as provide space for repair work and mechanic training; enlargement of the laundry building and a warehouse for storage purposes.

Besides growth in buildings, the institution has grown physically by the acquisition of another 244½ acre adjacent farm for the expansion of agricultural activity.

A second major accomplishment has been the growth of the State Use Industries program at the institution. In 1951 there was but one shop in operation, the cannery. In the course of eight years this has grown to seven shops (cannery, bookbindery, brush factory, feed mixing plant, metal-working shop, sewing shop and stone crushing project). Steps have been taken for the introduction of a poultry project in the near future.

Important expansion has taken place in the field of classification, with screening through new and improved tests, orientation programs, counseling and group therapy. Educational services have developed the program by being broadened both academically and vocationally.

Among the important innovations of the period has been the installation of a radio and sound system servicing all cells of the institution. Most recent among the improvements has been the provision for full time Chaplain services at the institution.

The Parole System

Under the Act of 1939, the Director of Parole, then a part-time official appointed every two years by the Governor, was also the Chairman of the Board of Parole. This Board consisted of the Chairman, the Attorney General, the Superintendent of Prisons and the Chief Probation Officer of the Supreme Bench of Baltimore City.

This Board served only as a policy making body and had nothing to do with the actual granting of parole. No person could be released on parole unless he or she was serving a term of one year or more and had served one-third of the sentence. The Director of Parole held hearings generally at the Parole Office in Annapolis, at which time any interested persons were permitted to appear before the Director to plead the case of the prisoner.

If the Director decided to recommend parole, the case was written up by the staff, and the home and employment program checked. The case then was transmitted to the Governor for his action. It was the Governor who had to grant the parole. The Governor was not bound by these recommendations. There was considerable delay in the handling of cases. There had been a growing feeling, however, that the inmate under consideration should be personally seen, and early in 1952, the first institutional hearings were scheduled at the Maryland Penitentiary.

The report of the Commission on Administrative Organization of the State, made in 1953, brought out the inadequacies of the parole system as it then existed. The Commission, which was appointed by Governor McKeldin, called for a complete revision of the parole system. Many organizations, both public and private, joined in an effort to secure the passage of this legislation; and after considerable discussion in the press and through the medium of radio and television, the Legislature passed the Parole Bill.

NEW PAROLE LAW

The new law, in addition to retaining the essential definitions of the old law, providing for the right of visitation and other matters pertaining to the operation of the Department, makes the following new provisions:

1. Creates a three-man Parole Board with six-year staggered terms. The Chairman is also the full-time Director and Administrator of the Department of Parole.

2. Places the power to grant paroles in a majority of the Board.

3. Eliminates the requirement that one-third of the sentence must be served prior to parole consideration.

4. Requires the Governor to consider and act upon the parole applications of life-termers after they have served at least 15 years.

5. Requires hearings at the various penal institutions with the prisoner present.

In addition to the provisions provided above, the new law permits cases to be heard regularly and to provide for rehearings when, in the opinion of the Board, such action is indicated. These rehearings are an important advance in the practice in Maryland.

The Board feels that, in many instances, persons admitted to parole should be required to make restitution, both because of the loss sustained and also for the therapeutic effect on the parolee. This policy has been carried out wherever feasible, and many thousands of dollars of restitution have been made.

Maryland now has established regular training programs for parole officers and has set up a Manual of Instructions on policy and supervisory practices which rates with the manuals of states which are regarded as leaders in the field of parole. The specifications for supervisory officers have been revised to include specialized study in the field of social science, and every applicant for a position in the category of parole officer is screened carefully to assure that he is morally and physically fit for this position.

PAROLE VIOLATORS HEARD

Under the law all prisoners returned for violation of parole must be granted a hearing before the Parole Board, and this policy has been carried out. However, the practice had been that hearings were attended only by the person under consideration, members of the Board, its staff and a member of the institutional staff. In 1957, however, the Court of Appeals held that an attorney has a right to attend a parole violation hearing, if requested by the parolee, and the Board now notifies each inmate of his right to be represented by counsel and secures from him a written statement concerning his desires in this regard, well in advance of the hearing date.

During this Administration integration of personnel was begun and continues to progress. In improving Departmental efficiency and in accomplishing the added responsibilities thrust upon the Department, it has been necessary to increase personnel and other facilities. While the personnel of the Department has not been increased in proportion to the added responsibility, sufficient increase has been afforded to achieve previously anticipated results for Departmental improvement. A system of classified application of supervision service known as Standards of Supervision has been adopted by the Board and applied in the supervision of all subjects.

RELEASES ON PAROLE

On January 1, 1951, the total caseload of the Department was 1,691 parolees and probationers, while in 1957, the caseload had risen to 3,529 parolees and probationers.

The records disclose that the cost of maintaining a prisoner in the penal institutions of the State is approximately $850 annually, while a cost of approximately $100 per year covers the cost of supervision of parolees and probationers.

Statistics available to the Department show that whereas in some states as high as 70% of those released from penal institutions are released on parole, the percentage of those released on parole in 1957 in Maryland was 29% of those who were given hearings. In the year 1950, the rate of release was 16.5%.

The State Police

Under Governor Theodore R. McKeldin's administration, the enforcement strength of the Department developed from 251 in 1951 to a present authorized strength of 471. Although the current estimated minimum requirement, based on recognized factors (traffic volume, persons killed, road mileage, etc.) is 629 and has not yet been achieved, the Governor's recognition of the importance of achieving it has brought it closer to reality than it has been at any time in the history of the Department.

Adjustments in salary ratios throughout the various ranks have increased the desirability of the position of State Trooper and eased the recruiting situation tremendously. Also, it has provided incentive for present police personnel to work toward promotion with its added responsibilities. The prior small difference in remuneration between some ranks had caused a serious decline in competition for promotion; the existence of such stagnation is injurious to any organization and particularly so to one dependent upon constant command development.

With increased enforcement personnel, available housing facilities became inadequate. New barracks are functioning at Cumberland and Waldorf; by May of 1958, the new Easton Barrack will be ready for occupancy, while negotiations are now under way and funds have been appropriated for the relocating of Conowingo Barrack in North East, due to a definite change in the traffic pattern. These are very satisfactory accomplishments under the Capital Improvement Program.

NEW POLICE ACADEMY

In 1951 foremost among Capital Improvements was the Police Academy project, for which Governor McKeldin broke ground on March 23, 1953. On March 29, 1954, he dedicated the building and since seven recruit schools have been graduated, putting into active duty two hundred and thirty-nine troopers.

Since its inception, the Academy staff has provided training services for numerous law enforcement agencies.

The construction of the Academy represented the third quarter of the quadrangle of buildings at Headquarters. It is anticipated that the final quarter—a building which would house the Central Accident Records Bureau now at Guilford Avenue and 21st Street, and the Mess Hall—soon would be placed under construction.

The Department has agreed to incorporate in this facility space to accommodate the Maryland and Civil Defense Agency. Funds have been appropriated to the Maryland State Police and to the Maryland Civil Defense Agency under the Capital Improvements Program, with some matching Federal funds for this installation. Architecturally, it is in the planning stages.

AIR ARM

During the present administration the Department acquired its first airplane. This since has been traded for a new aircraft providing the Department with a more adequate air search and traffic control vehicle. The services of this craft have been exceptionally gratifying on several occasions and proved economical in many ways.

The Department's motor vehicle fleet increased from 244 in 1951 to 424 as of now. Motorcycle units, because of the connected hazards, have been reduced to four.

In keeping with modern methods of enforcement, the Department since 1951 has acquired ten radar units, providing one unit for each barrack. They are in constant use throughout the State, providing impersonal and factual means of enforcement. They are not used to obtain great number of arrests, but mainly to control speeds through areas where excessive speeding seems to become a problem periodically.

In addition to Headquarters, the nine barracks and College Park, radio communication posts have been installed at Centreville, Crisfield, Prince Frederick, Leonardtown, Rockville and Hagerstown.

Relocation of Route 40 over Polish Mountain. The cut—147 feet—is the deepest in Maryland.

Funds have been appropriated and bids requested for the construction of a radio maintenance shop at the Waterloo Barrack, Radio Division Headquarters.

AMBULANCE SERVICE

Ambulances have been replaced at each barrack with a carry-all ambulance, with equipment installed by Departmental personnel.

Fifteen auxiliary emergency generators have been installed at our various posts to provide power in the event of regular power failure, enabling the Department to maintain vital communications operations.

Two mobile generators are available for the supply of emergency power.

Seven buildings housing radio transmitter equipment were constructed at Westminster, Gambrills Park, Salisbury, Bel Air, Dan's Mountain, Woodlawn and High Nob—as well as establishment of a post at Rockville with radio communications. Five of these, in their entirety or in part, were constructed by Departmental personnel.

The overall project represented a substantial financial savings to this Department and the State by several thousands of dollars. One hundred and forty-two mobile radio units and six barrack receivers were purchased when the Department changed over to a two-frequency operation.

Space does not permit enumeration of all State Police accomplishments, but a few of the outstanding follow:

The Department successfully handled two major riots in the prison system during 1953 and 1954 (Women's Prison—Reformatory for Males).

The Libertytown (Md.) bank was robbed on July 10, 1953. Three subjects apprehended by our Department within thirteen minutes following the hold-up were convicted of the crime and are serving long prison sentences.

On July 7, 1954, five desperate criminals escaped from the Marlboro Jail. Within a few hours, three of these subjects were apprehended by our Department.

In May of 1957, a patient with homicidal tendencies escaped from the Springfield State Hospital. Apprehension of this mentally sick person was made quickly and without harm to the subject through use of the Department aircraft.

DISASTER AID

The Department responded, cooperated and coordinated their efforts with other units by assisting in the rescue of survivors, the injured, indentification of the dead, traffic control and direction, evacuation and transportation to shelter areas and utilizing to a maximum its communication and other emergency facilities at the scene of the following disasters:

Kent Manufacturing Company Explosion
Chestertown, Maryland
July 16, 1954
Resulted in the death of eleven persons—serious injuries to five and lesser injuries to forty others.

Hurricane Hazel
October 15, 1954

Sinking of the Schooner—"Levin J. Marvel"
August 12, 1955
Sank in the Chesapeake Bay with a loss of fourteen lives during a raging storm.

Pennsylvania Railroad Train Wreck
Odenton, Maryland
February 23, 1956
Resulted in the loss of six lives and injuries to scores of persons.

This Department has received national recognition for participation in the Crash Injury Research Project instituted in cooperation with Cornell Medical College and the Medical Chirurgical Society of Maryland.

The Department, by virtue of its duties is an important factor in Civil Defense—therefore, cooperation and coordination with the Maryland Civil Defense Agency is vital. The two agencies, pooling their resources, developed and completed an effective radio network in case of disaster. The Federal Government assisted in the financing of this project.

Headquarters at Pikesville is the Alert Center for the State of Maryland. In the event of a national emergency, the communications network will be of paramount importance.

The Department, in cooperation with the Maryland Civil Defense Agency and the Baltimore Area Survival Project, developed a detailed traffic control plan to accomplish an evacuation of the Baltimore and Washington areas, if necessary.

Despite the importance of its work in crime prevention, crime detection, and in disasters and other major police functions, the Department's most important day-by-day and night-by-night activity is the patrol of the State's growing system of highways, the prevention of traffic violations where possible, the apprehension of violators where necessary, the prevention of accidents and the giving of general assistance to the motoring public.

Maryland Traffic Safety Commission

In 1941 the Maryland Traffic Safety Commission was organized to promote traffic safety in the State of Maryland by means of Traffic Safety Education. This program required the cooperation of every media of public information.

Prior to 1951 Maryland ranked quite low among the States in the field of Public Safety Education. But in 1955 Maryland received First Award and since then has ranked with the leaders as determined by the National Safety Council.

The Commission, in its education program, showed films before interested groups, distributed printed materials, posters and billboards, and members and staff address civic, fraternal and other groups.

These figures of the National Safety Council illustrate the success of the program in cooperation with police and other officials, private organizations, individuals, press, radio and television.

Year	*Maryland Mileage Death Rate*	*National Average*
1950	7.6 persons	7.5 persons
1951	7.8 persons	7.6 persons
1952	7.0 persons	7.3 persons
1953	6.5 persons	7.0 persons
1954	6.3 persons	6.4 persons
1955	5.7 persons	6.4 persons
1956	5.7 persons	6.4 persons
1957	5.4 persons	5.9 persons

Studies to date have shown that the downward trend will continue through 1958. The above figures are based upon the death rate per 100 million miles of travel in Maryland. The success of Maryland in holding the line on traffic fatalities has been recognized by both the National Safety Council and the American Automobile Association. Governor McKeldin has been presented with twelve National Awards for the State in public acknowledgment of the activities of the Commission.

Listed below is a sampling of the activities which merited this consideration:

Year	*Literature Distributed*	*Posters Distributed*	*Safety Speeches*	*Press Releases*	*Film Showings*
1953	10,460,000	84,000	7,101	5,137	3,621
1955	17,960,000	78,000	10,122	8,667	4,814

In addition to the above, the Maryland Traffic Safety Commission conducted interviews, distributed news and feature mats, produced spot announcements for radio and television, solicited and received many hours of radio and television time from the stations throughout Maryland and sponsored in the schools a child safety program. The Commission also assisted the Automobile Club of Maryland to create interest in school boy and girl safety, was the driving force behind the "S-D Day" campaign instigated by the President of the United States and spearheaded in Maryland the "*Slow Down and Live*" safety campaign entreating the vacationing public to drive safely.

The Maryland Traffic Safety Commission assisted the members of the Maryland General Assembly in their efforts to improve the safety of highway users in the State and cooperated with all the State agencies charged with the movement and regulation of pedestrian and vehicular traffic.

State Accident Fund

The Annotated Code of Maryland, Article 101, Section 68, provides that there shall be a "State Accident Fund" for the purpose of insuring employers against liability under Article 101, which is the Workmen's Compensation Law of Maryland, and to their employees and their dependents the payment of compensation specified.

During the present State Administration, the State Accident Fund has enjoyed spectacular growth and success in fulfilling its obligations as shown by the following six-year operational comparison.

	Reserves	*Premiums Written*	*Number of Accidents Reported*	*Number of Policies In Effect*	*Claims Paid to Injured Workmen*
1951	$4,457,412.34	$1,026,984.29	8,622	3,641	$ 784,861.20
1957	$7,269,286.26	$2,084,850.31	11,977	4,529	$1,678,303.99

During this same period the State Legislature has liberalized the Compensation Laws of the State of Maryland. This has, of necessity, greatly increased the cost of compensation insurance. In spite of these substantial increases in benefits the State Accident Fund has been able to provide prompt and sympathetic service to its policyholders and their employees. At the same time it has strengthened the financial reserves of the Fund so that at the present time its reserves are adequate and the Fund appears to be established on a firm and sound basis.

It has been the policy of the State Accident Fund to accept for insurance any legitimate business activity, regardless of hazards involved, requiring employment in the State of Maryland. During the years that the Fund has been in operation, it has never declined to accept any risk offered. It has relied for protection against loss on accident prevention programs, calculated to train employees in the most modern safety practices as well as a premium incentive plan which has materially rewarded those businesses that have protected their employees and prevented accidents.

Operations during the fiscal year 1956-1957 resulted in substantial increases in the reserves of the State Accident Fund. These reserves were attained through the effectiveness of our safety program and the close cooperation of the many employers insured in the Fund. In order to suitably recognize those firms who were mainly responsible for this success, the Commissioners of the Fund declared an additional merit dividend based upon each firm's established merit rating.

All of the above has been accomplished without cost to the taxpayers of the State of Maryland. The State Accident Fund is a self-supporting institution, deriving its entire revenue from commissions charged the various policyholders and interest received from the investment of its surplus accounts. The remarkable growth and expansion of services during the last several years has been largely attributable to the close cooperation and interest the Commissioners have received from Governor McKeldin, the State Legislature and the Budget Bureau.

Workman's Compensation Commission

In 1957 the Legislature completely reorganized the State Industrial Accident Commission Act and in its place created the new body known as the Workman's Compensation Commission.

The Commissioners, under the new Act, became full-time State employees. The old body operated on a part-time basis, thus amassing a large backlog of pending cases. Already, through the addition of another hearing room and the commissioners sitting all day, inroads have been made in reducing this backlog.

The Legislature, in 1951, substantially increased the number of employee classifications covered under the old Act and also eliminated the specific schedule of "occupational diseases." This substantially increased the work load of the Commission and it has continued to rise.

The expansion of industry, requiring large numbers of additional employees, logically has increased the number of claims before the Commission.

A sweeping revision of the Commission's schedule for medical and surgical fees was made in 1951. The raising of the fees resulted in much more detailed hearings, thereby taking more time.

In the same year a study was made of the financial resources of self-insurers to check their responsibility.

COMMISSION MEMBERS INCREASED

The Legislature, in 1952, amended the Workman's Compensation Act, increasing the membership of the Commission from four to five Commissioners.

Subsequently, the Commission, in order to expedite the handling of claims, revised the various forms for the necessary paper work. This resulted in accelerating the movement of claims.

AMENDED IN 1955

The Compensation Act was amended again in 1955. At this time the Safety Department was removed from the Commission and transferred to the Department of Labor and Industry.

The Commission always has worked closely with the Division of Vocational Rehabilitation, and through their combined efforts a further service was made available to the handicapped worker. In July, 1955, all insurance carriers, self-insurers and the State Accident Fund were notified of the Commission's new policy covering prosthesis.

Employers were informed that wherever a prosthesis was ordered by the Commission, medical treatment should include training in the use of such device at the insurer's expense.

The 1957 Legislature gave the claimant the right to elect where his claim should be heard. He could choose the county where the alleged accident occurred, the county where the employee lived at the time of the accident or in Baltimore City. This will add to the traveling time of the Hearing Commissioners sitting in the various counties.

BENEFITS INCREASED

Benefits allowed claimants have been increased materially in recent years. Death benefits have risen from $7,500 to $10,000; funeral expenses up from $300 to $500 and total disability awards from $7,500 to $20,000. The ceiling has been removed from awards for medical expenses and the amount of the benefits now is unlimited.

Department of Public Welfare

The seven year span from 1951 to 1957, inclusive, were on the whole prosperous years in the State of Maryland. Except for one year when there was a slight recession in business activity, employment was at a peace-time high and there were a minimal number of people receiving public assistance. However, this minimal number represented a large group of individuals. During December 1957 there were 53,272 men, women and children receiving part or all of their basic maintenance from the State welfare program.

During a year there is a turnover of approximately 40% in cases assisted, so that something around 70,000 Marylanders for some period during 1957 received financial assistance under the State public welfare law. In addition to giving financial assistance and service under the public assistance and child care programs, the Welfare Department engaged in numerous other activities.

The welfare program of the State is divided roughly into four categories: Public Assistance; Foster Care; Services to the Young Delinquent and Miscellaneous Services.

PUBLIC ASSISTANCE

Public Assistance in Maryland is administered by the 23 County Welfare Boards and the Department of Public Welfare in Baltimore

City, under the supervision and direction of the State Department of Public Welfare. Public Assistance means a money grant once a month to an individual or family in need for food, clothing, shelter, etc., where there is no resource.

Public Assistance is divided into five categories: Old Age Assistance; Aid to the Needy Blind; Aid to the Permanently and Totally Disabled; Aid to Dependent Children and General Public Assistance.

The Maryland program is one of the least expensive in the nation.

There have been certain changes upwards in standards over the last seven years, but the most notable increase was in the grant made for nursing care. With the increasing number of older people who need convalescent care and with a limited number of State chronic hospital beds, the effort has been made to have private capital go into the field of nursing homes, and secondly, to raise the level of service given by nursing homes up to a more adequate level of patient care. The State is now paying a grant not to exceed $120 a month for all items for the larger areas of the State, and not to exceed $110 a month for the more rural areas. This is less than the amount that is necessary to anywhere near solve the problem, but it represents distinct progress.

FOSTER CARE

The overwhelming majority of these children are committed to the local welfare departments by the courts of the State on the ground of neglect; and as of December 31, 1957 there were 4,757 children in care. This means that the local welfare departments have actually found a home for the child with a family, or else are paying for his care with a private agency or institution. There seems to be a constant rise in the number of commitments.

During the seven year span notable progress has been made in the area of adoption. The State Department of Welfare now administers a central pool where children from one unit of government who are adoptable are placed and can be adopted by couples living in other subdivisions. This gives to the child a much better chance of proper placement. The number of children benefited by the adoption program has had a wide expansion over the period. During 1958 it is estimated that arrangements will be made for the adoption of over 250 children in the care of the program.

SERVICES TO THE YOUNG DELINQUENT

The services that the State renders to the young delinquent are perhaps on a less satisfactory basis than the other services rendered by the public to children from tax funds. Certainly, the public school program, many of the health services to children, and the foster care program are more satisfactory than the services rendered to the young delinquent. It was because of this that the Commission on Administrative Organization of the State, appointed in 1951, directed particular attention to the young delinquent and found existing programs to be confused and inadequate.

The other side of the problem is that Maryland is a rapidly growing State and there are literally thousands and thousands of new children. In addition to this, the number of children getting into difficulty with the law per thousand throughout the country has been increasing. This means that there will be additional children committed to the schools each year within the foreseeable future.

To meet the need for the additional children the main resource has been to cut down on the average time which the child stays in the institution. For the boys' schools this has now been reduced to less than a year. In addition to this the Legislature has authorized three forestry camps. Two are now in operation, and one is in the process of being constructed. These will provide resources for something between 80 and 90 additional children.

NEW COMMISSION

Even more important for children than juvenile courts and training schools are the things that happen to children which cause delinquency prior to any contact with a law enforcement agency. For this reason, among others, the Governor appointed in the Spring of 1956 a State Commission on the Prevention and Treatment of Juvenile Delinquency. The staff of the Division of Consultant and Prevention Services of the State Welfare Department staff the Commission.

The Commission consists of some 35 members and has active subcommittees involving over 200 different Marylanders from the various disciplines working with children and from all geographical areas of the State. The Commission has held two Statewide two-day Conferences on Juvenile Delinquency at the University of Maryland, with an average attendance of in excess of 500 interested persons, and is in the process of drawing up a plan for the future in the field of children's services.

Studies have been made of the effectiveness of probation departments in various counties, and in one county the recommendations were used by a very able Juvenile Court Judge in his efforts to set up a much more effective probation department. Other studies have been made in other counties at the request of County Commissioners and judges. Consulting services have also been given to various counties in meeting miscellaneous problems presented by children.

Montrose School

There have been many changes and improvements at Montrose during the years since 1951. The program for girls has been broadened in scope and deepened in the therapeutic and individualized approach to disturbed girls and their problems. More girls come to the school each year, but the capacity remains the same, so the service must be more intensive, in order to help each girl in a shorter period of time. In 1951, there was 248 committed children, 75 detained children; in 1957 there were 251 committed and 125 detained children. In 1951 the average girl stayed two years, in 1957 she stayed ten months. Increased efficiency in the running of the school means that a comparable service is being given in a shorter period of time.

Nearly a half million dollars have been spent at Montrose since 1951 in much needed additions, repairs and improvements.

Among the largest individual expenditures were those for a new sewage treatment plant and additional water facilities. These projects were most necessary for health and sanitation. There was construction of much needed dormitories and improvements to those extant.

The heating facilities have been brought to top efficiency both by new installations and extensive repairs and improvements.

A new classroom building was constructed, a big step in the educational program.

The following areas of the school program have been changed to meet today's needs:

1. Cottage life program has been stabilized in personnel and enriched in content. Women of character and quality have been attracted to and have stayed in the housemother positions—their contribution to girls is too great to measure.

2. A professional social casework department has been developed to meet the needs of girls and their families. More intensive casework is being done in order that personality changes can be effected in our charges, more individualized care and treatment are being given. Students from leading schools of social work are now being trained in this department.

3. After-care supervision has been taken over by the local Departments of Welfare or community agencies. This has resulted in a more efficient service as people in the local community become responsible for

helping girls move out of the school and assume their responsibilities as citizens of the larger community. It has made it possible for the case work staff of the school to concentrate on the needs of the school population and helped in the development of a more individualized therapeutic approach to the treatment of the girls.

4. The educational program has been enriched; its whole aim and philosophy modified to meet the current situation. Music was added to the curriculum, the Art and Craft program was developed to a higher level, a library which girls enjoy using has been built up, policies around grade placement have been modified to better serve the needs of the students and special educational methods have been adopted to meet the needs of educationally retarded girls. The school building was renovated to fit the changing program; presently an addition is being built to accommodate the vocational classrooms. There have been tremendous changes and growth in our school program.

5. During 1956 and 1957 our staff was integrated; from a small start the policy has been broadened to include all positions. Staff live and work in harmony and are teaching children to think and practice democratic principles of living. As these things are summarized into a few brief sentences, it seems less important than the struggle which brought them about. Integration was accomplished easily—yet, is was preceded by such resistance on the part of staff and students that it seemed impossible to ever have the two groups living and working together in our small school where relationships are fewer and therefore much closer. The years between 1951 and 1958 have been years of progress for Montrose.

Boys' Village

Prior to nine years ago there were frequent changes in school administration, competent staff members could not be recruited, buildings had deteriorated beyond the point where renovation was possible.

More children absconded from the institution yearly than were committed. Today, approximately nine years after one of the darkest periods in any children's institution's history almost all criticism has vanished. Only one of the original six dilapidated youths' cottages still remains. More than 2½ million dollars have been spent during this time on new buildings, equipment, steam lines and other improvements.

Some of the new structures include nine new cottages and each houses twenty-five boys as well as provides quarters for two staff couples. There is also a new oil fueled boiler house, a new central kitchen-vocational shop building, several new farm structures, intercommunication system, new well, pumps, and pump houses, new administration building, a recently developed reservoir which is also used as a farm fish pond, twelve quonset apartments for the staff. In addition $400,000 has been allotted for a new classroom building which will be attached to the present gymnasium; and $270,000 is available for a new staff dormitory to house forty-eight staff members which will be completed within less than a year.

During the past eight years several surveys conducted by educational and social work authorities have described the services for delinquent children as superior in many respects. Staff morale has continued high; it is difficult to recruit stable, qualified personnel who understand and are liked by children. There are few children's institutions in the country where the "run-away" rate is as low as at Boys' Village.

Barrett School for Girls

Since 1951, great strides have been made in improvements to the physical plant of the school. During this period more than $123,000 has been expended for this purpose.

The three largest expenditures were devoted to much needed improvements for health, safety and sanitation. More than $22,000 was allocated to a new Dispensary building and more than $15,000 each was allotted to installation of fire escapes and renovations of the sewage system.

In the past few years the morale of the resident girls has improved materially. The same can be said for the staff and has been reflected in much greater stability.

The resident population of the school has risen from 51 in 1954 to the present 73. The all-time high of 84 was reached earlier this year.

Also, seven new staff positions were created which brings the administrative personnel to a total of 49.

Training School for Boys

In 1951 the Maryland Training School for Boys found itself faced with almost insurmountable problems. Overcrowding in the cottages of the School resulting from the closing of St. Mary's School and shortages in personnel resulted in an explosive situation culminating in an investigation of the Management of the School.

Today the School still finds itself confronted with population pressures, but during the intervening years real strides have been taken by the State to add much needed facilities. Six additional cottage units have been completed. To serve the increased population, a service building was constructed replacing antiquated kitchen, laundry, and storeroom facilities.

A renovation of several of the older cottage units to replace outmoded sanitary facilities and make much needed repairs was completed. From the standpoint of safety, necessary fire escapes and other fire protection measures were undertaken. Apartments for cottage staff were enlarged and remodeled and a residence for the Assistant Superintendent constructed.

The needs of an expanded program in the educational area were met by the construction of a ten-classroom elementary school building, while the School's religious program was augmented by the renovation of the chapel. One of the most necessary projects covered during this period of growth is the McKeldin Gymnasium-Auditorium which made possible, for the first time in many years, a fully organized recreational program. Its large gym floor and facilities for boxing, wrestling, weightlifting and other indoor sports have enriched the recreational program manyfold.

In total cost the building program completed in this institution during this period of time is valued at over $2,000,000.

GROWTH IN PERSONNEL

Part of the substantial growth in the School's personnel allotment can be traced to the much needed reduction in the State work week from 48 to 44, and later to 40 hours weekly. But more importantly the increase has inflicted a growing conviction that money spent for the professional staff required to rehabilitate delinquent boys is money wisely spent. Major areas of an improved treatment program are reflected in the increase in professional staff.

From a 1951 staff composed of nine teachers, the educational program has developed into a twenty-three teacher program meeting the needs of children from elementary through high school subjects. In the vital area of clinical services, a similar expansion has taken place. A total of eleven new positions have been added to this division representing a doubling of medical personnel. New elements of program were introduced as a result, including a social work student program in collaboration with the School of Social Work of the Catholic University which has done much to stimulate the professional advancement of the casework staff.

The addition of full time Protestant and Catholic chaplains has filled a vital need in the lives of the boys of the School. It is especially noteworthy also that the School has taken real strides in integrating its staff and the School has among its staff a number of well qualified Negro teachers and caseworkers.

The growth in professional staff has resulted in real and substantial improvements in the School's program for delinquent boys.

GROWTH IN PROGRAM

The construction of new cottage facilities made possible for the first time a separation in the program offered younger and older boys within the School's population. The new cottage units have been organized into a program for the younger boys separating them completely from the older, more sophisticated population. With the construction of the elementary school building, the younger boys no longer have any contact with the older population of the School except during religious services and school-wide assemblies.

Prior to the expansion of the clinical staff, the Training School had depended primarily upon a grading system to determine the eligibility of boys for return to the community. The School has now been able to move towards a clinical evaluation of each boy's readiness for return, in which careful consideration is given to psychological and psychiatric diagnosis as well as to social history and other information concerning each boy's individual abilities and progress within the School program.

Such a program makes it possible for a boy to be returned to the community at the point when he is most ready to do so. It has resulted in a substantial reduction in the average length of stay. At the present time the average length of stay for committed boys within the Training School is between eight and nine months, which the School believes an irreducible minimum in consonance with acceptable release standards.

As the School's program moved toward a treatment approach, certain aspects of its former program were examined and it was felt wise to curtail them. The School's military system in which the population was organized into military companies and boys were placed in position of leadership took unfair advantage of their position to work a hardship on other students. With the abandonment of the system much less problem of this nature has existed.

The School has developed programs in almost every sport and has fielded varsity teams in the major sports. Boys from the School participated in the boxing and basketball tournaments of the South Atlantic Conference. Varsity baseball and wrestling teams are in competition with local clubs. An extensive program of inter-cottage tournaments in the major sports has been instrumental in fostering good morale and developing qualities of team play and sportsmanship which are essential in the rehabilitation of the delinquent.

An expanded program of visits to the State Capitol and other historical points within the state has also been of excellent merit in acquainting the boys with the history and traditions of the Free State. The School's traditional Christmas Pageant and June Day Open House have been substantially improved, while a new Easter Program is currently under preparation. The School is proud of its greatly expanded recreational program and recognizes it as one of the primary tools of rehabilitation.

The record of progress made during the years 1951-1958 is one of which the citizens of Maryland can justly be proud. The state program for delinquent youths as represented in the Maryland Training School for Boys has been improved immeasurably due both to expanded physical and staff growth.

The Board of Natural Resources

The Board of Natural Resources coordinates the activities of five State Departments concerned with conservation and administration of resources. They are the Department of Tidewater Fisheries, the Department of Game and Inland Fish, the Department of Forests and Parks, the Department of Geology, Mines and Water Resources, and the Department of Research and Education.

MARYLAND'S HISTORIC BOUNDARIES

The east-west line between Maryland and Delaware was laid out by colonial surveyors in 1751 when Delaware was still a part of Pennsylvania. As the survey progressed, the line was marked at five-mile intervals by monuments of native stone carved with the Penn coat of arms on the Pennsylvania side and the Calvert coat of arms on the Maryland side. The north-south line between Maryland and Delaware and the east-west line between Maryland and Pennsylvania were surveyed by Charles Mason and Jeremiah Dixon during the period 1763-1767. The two lines surveyed by Mason and Dixon were marked at one-mile intervals by stone monuments imported from England. Every fifth stone was engraved with the Penn coat of arms on the Pennsylvania side and the Calvert coat of arms on the Maryland side. Monuments between succeeding "crown-stones" were marked with an M on the Maryland side and a P on the Pennsylvania side.

The Board of Natural Resources inspected and photographed the markers on these three boundaries in 1950 and 1951. A report on the condition of the markers was submitted at the beginning of the McKeldin administration.

The report stated that the Maryland-Delaware boundaries had been completely neglected for nearly two centuries. Many of the markers on these two boundaries were broken or otherwise damaged, some had been removed from their correct position and a few had been lost.

The legislatures of Maryland and Delaware passed complementary acts enabling the Board of Natural Resources and the corresponding agencies in Delaware to cooperate in the restoration of the historic boundaries between the States. At the request of the Board and its colleagues in Delaware, the Congress passed an act directing the U. S. Coast and Geodetic Survey to resurvey the north-south line between Maryland and

Delaware and to correct or confirm the position of each of the markers installed by Mason and Dixon. The two States now await the resurvey. When this is completed, the Board and corresponding officials of Delaware will repair and reset the Mason and Dixon boundary markers which have been neglected for nearly two hundred years.

PUBLICATIONS ON THE NATURAL RESOURCES

Early in the present administration, Governor McKeldin and the Board of Public Works provided the Board with a special revolving fund to enable it to supply schools, libraries and the general public with publications on Maryland resources. The revolving fund permits the Board to maintain a stock of State conservation publications which are sold at cost. Receipts from sales are credited to the fund and are used to print new items or to revise and reprint depleted stocks of old publications. The revolving fund has been highly successful. When the revolving fund was established, outline maps for school use were available only from out-of-State publishers at five cents each. The Board now annually supplies schools with about 25,000 such maps printed in Maryland at a cost of one cent each. Most of the Board's publications are sold to Maryland schools and libraries, but materials have been shipped as far as Kenya and South Rhodesia.

THE DAM AT LITTLE FALLS

Early in the present administration the Board of Natural Resources learned that the U. S. Corps of Engineers, on behalf of the Commissioners of the District of Columbia, proposed to construct a dam at Little Falls on the Potomac River to replace an old dam built in 1831 to operate locks on the C & O Canal. The purpose of the new dam was to provide a water supply for the District of Columbia and for nearby communities in Maryland and Virginia.

The commercial fishermen of the lower Potomac River capture annually millions of pounds of shad, herring, striped bass and other migratory fish which spawn each year in the upper Potomac River. Unless the proposed dam were provided with a fishway, migratory fish would be permanently excluded from important spawning and nursery grounds between Little Falls and Great Falls, a distance of approximately ten miles.

The Board of Natural Resources urged that the new dam be provided with a fishway which would be an integral part of the dam and be financed like the dam itself. When the General Assembly became aware of the situation, an act was passed authorizing the Board to require a fishway on dams such as that proposed at Little Falls. When this act was

Opening of Chesapeake Bay oyster season.

called to the attention of the District of Columbia and the Corps of Engineers, the Board of Natural Resources was advised that federal agencies are immune to State laws.

Senators Butler and Beall and Representative Hyde became staunch allies of the Board, and with the support of other Maryland congressmen, the U. S. Fish and Wildlife Service, the conservation agencies of Virginia, the National Wildlife Federation and a number of other local and national conservation agencies, an appropriation was made by the Congress for the fishway at Little Falls.

THE WATER CHESTNUT

Early in 1955 the Board was advised by the U. S. Fish and Wildlife Service that beds of the water chestnut, *Trapa natans,* had become established in the Gunpowder River. This plant is a pernicious weed which spreads rapidly, chokes out more desirable aquatic vegetation, impedes navigation, harbors mosquitoes and produces spiny seeds which are ruinous to bathing beaches.

No funds were available for the control of the water chestnut. On the advice of the Board, the Department of Tidewater Fisheries, the Department of Game and Inland Fish and the Department of Forests and Parks in the summer of 1955 mustered a small field crew and assembled appropriate equipment on the Gunpowder River.

These men, with no previous experience and almost no instruction, organized themselves into a highly effective task force for an attack on the water chestnut. The same methods were employed in succeeding summers. The encouragement of the Board and the interest and cooperation of the field crew now have reduced the water chestnut to a few scattered plants. A similar outbreak of this pest in the Potomac River in the 1930's had cost the federal government nearly a million dollars.

QUARTERS FOR STATE CONSERVATION AGENCIES

Since the creation of the Board of Natural Resources in 1941, the Board and its associated departments had been widely separated geographically. The Board and two departments have been located in Annapolis, two departments have been housed in Baltimore and the fifth department has maintained headquarters at Solomons. In February, 1956, the Board itself was compelled to move from the State Office Building in Annapolis to rented quarters in a vacant restaurant.

The Board and four of its five component departments now are housed in the new State Office Building in Annapolis.

The Department of Forests and Parks

A rising population and expanding urbanization have brought new pressures on the State's outdoor recreation facilities and on the services of forest and park personnel.

Since 1951, we have been expanding State park areas through gifts of land and by purchase; by recovery of Federal resettlement lands, and by dedication to recreation purposes of State-owned forest lands.

Maryland has a two-fold forestry goal:

1. Scientific management for the multiple use of forests on critical watersheds, in cooperation with other agencies and the public.
2. Restoration of the volume and quality of the forest growth that once made Maryland a major source of supply for forest products in the eastern markets.

Under the Forest Conservancy Act of 1943, the State controls all commercial forest operations to the extent of preventing devastation cuttings. This phase of the law is administered by County Forestry Conservancy Boards, working with the State Forester for the district.

Free technical advice is furnished on request to forest land owners, and certain operating services are provided at nominal cost.

Of the 271 new calls for such assistance in the past year, 92 resulted in the marking of trees suitable for current sale or use. From such markings, 5,942,174 board feet of lumber were sold, providing $156,109 in cash income to the owners.

Results are cumulative and much of the timber sold each year from private lands is cut in accordance with management plans and patterns previously recommended.

Land owners are encouraged to engage private consultant foresters where available. Foresters employed by industrial companies also cooperate.

The Department, during the past year, received 648 requests to make recommendations for tree planting on 4,069 acres of watershed area.

The Department now manages 121,144 acres of State Forests and 15,564 acres of State Parks.

In several areas, watershed improvements and maintenance are the basic objectives, with the Department serving as an advisory agency to the Water Resources Commission established by Governor McKeldin in 1955.

SPECIAL FORESTRY PROJECT

The Eastern Shore Forest Improvement Project is aimed primarily at the reestablishment of loblolly pine as a profitable, marketable product of the Shore.

The Department has conducted the basic research for the project in cooperation with the Federal Northeastern Forest Experiment Station.

FOREST FIRE CONTROL

Maryland ranks among the leading States in forest fire control.

In 1950, 632 fires involved damage to .11 per cent of the forest area, with timber loss of more than $17,000. The State and the Counties spent $11,000 in fighting the fires.

In 1957, there were 452 fires, with a loss of only .055 per cent of the forest land. Timber damage amounted to less than $9,000. The State and the Counties spent $14,345 in the firefighting.

FORESTRY SERVICE

Since the beginning of the present Administration, the State has repossessed 47,832 acres of land from the Federal Government. The land is being planted where necessary and otherwise developed for forestry purposes.

Forest products sold from State lands have an annual value of about $30,000.

Extensive research is conducted into planting, growing and harvesting.

Production of planting stock at the Forest Nursery at Harmans is from about a million seedlings a year to more than six million.

STATE PARKS

Since 1951, State Park acreage has been tripled—from 5,305 acres to 15,761. This will expand to 17,000 acres or more.

Under the McKeldin program, five new parks were created and seven others extended in the seven-year period.

Patapsco River Valley Park, launched in the present Administration, has 4,446 acres and will expand to 7,800 acres.

In Montgomery County, 225 acres have been added to the original 50 in Seneca State Park.

The first Maryland Ocean Front Park—Assateague in Worcester County—covers 540 acres.

Southern Maryland is getting its first State park in an area dedicated to the memory of General W. M. Smallwood of Revolutionary fame.

There is progress in the planning of a new woodland park in the valleys of the Gunpowder and Little Gunpowder Rivers.

One of many newly-built roadside parks.

Additionally, more than 1,000 acres acquired and more than 1,200 under option on South Mountain in Frederick and Washington Counties, although specified as watershed area, will have well-kept trails and other developments for recreational use.

There were more than four million visits to State Parks and Forests during the past year—not counting hunters. Picnicking is the most popular use, but the parks and the forest recreation areas also are used extensively for organization and community group meetings, field games and hiking.

The demand for park and recreation areas will grow with our expanding population and the easy access created by a good system of roads.

Department of Tidewater Fisheries

Management of the aquatic resources of Tidewater Maryland is a highly complex business. In the Chesapeake Bay and its tributaries with their varying depths and salt content and in the Sinepuxent Bay and Atlantic Ocean off Worcester County flourish innumerable species of animal and plant life. Some are directly of importance, furnishing much of the economy of the fifteen bordering Counties in the harvesting, processing and marketing of seafood; others are indirectly so; while many more are without commercial value.

Here fish and crabs migrate freely; fishing methods vary and sometimes conflict with each other. A propitious season for oyster breeding may be followed by one of strong spring freshets that harmfully change the water salinity. Any number of natural phenomena may influence the production and growth of seafood.

In direct proportion to the steady increase in populations of people are the demands made upon our natural resources to supply their needs.

It is the regulation and control of these natural aquatic resources of commerce and recreation with which the Commission of Tidewater Fisheries and its subordinate Department of Tidewater Fisheries are charged. Notwithstanding the many perplexities encountered, since 1951 the Commission, through the Department, has made notable progress.

LAW ENFORCEMENT

The present Commission of Tidewater Fisheries, in 1951, recognized law enforcement to be the first essential to effective conservation.

Today the Department's Marine Patrol and Inspection Force is a far cry from the "Oyster Navy" of not too long ago—a heterogeneous collection of antiquated sail and motor boats, whose crews, untrained ununiformed and poorly qualified, were recruited at the opening of each oyster season and discharged at its close.

Under the direction of the present Commission, service in the Force has become a career profession. The Commission has prescribed stringent basic requirements for recruitment in the Force. The curriculum of the training course embraces a wide variety of required subjects for a superior police officer. Members of the Federal Bureau of Investigation usually serve on its faculty.

Modern patrol craft specifically designed or selected for the task of law enforcement have replaced the antiquated fleet.

Patrol cars have been added to supplement the effectiveness of the patrol fleet. A seaplane with a competent pilot performs reconnaissance duty. Boats, cars and plane are linked together to the Headquarters of the Department and to the Maryland State Police by two-way mobile radios over which constant and reliable communication is maintained.

Each inspector wears a regulation uniform bearing insignia distinguishing him as a police officer.

Characteristic of the Force is the "A-1" rating granted in 1957 by the United States Public Health Service for outstanding merit in preventing the harvesting of polluted seafood.

OYSTER CULTURE

In the season of 1954-55 the oyster harvest rose, from the low to which it had declined, to above the three million bushel mark to reach its highest peak in fifteen years.

This outstanding success may be attributed to:

1. The "fifty per cent law" of 1951, returning to public bars one-half the shells generated each season throughout the State.

2. An oyster propagation program of carefully selected bars for rehabilitation by shell planting and/or seeding, improved techniques to insure the even distribution of shell and seed, mechanization of the processes, purchase of added quantities of shells over and above the State's fifty per cent, surveying and sampling, restricting or closing of given areas to promote breeding and growth.

3. Making seed oysters available to private planters—278,856 bushels from State-owned areas since 1951.

4. Increasing the acreage of barren bottom leased to private planters —more than 1,400 added acres.

Notwithstanding such catastrophes as hurricanes, the Commission has been able to maintain the oyster yield on a constant, stable level.

SOFT SHELL CLAM INDUSTRY

In 1951 the Soft Shell Clam industry was in its infancy. Figures of the United States Fish and Wildlife Service place the 1953 catch at 315,000 pounds of clam meat. The same source shows the 1955 figure to be 1,293,720 pounds, representing, over the two-year period, an increase of more than 310 per cent.

The Commission has been instrumental in stabilizing this industry to insure its permanency and growth through beneficial controls which have eliminated much of the early controversy with which the industry was greeted.

ROCKFISH INVESTIGATION

The Rockfish Investigation was undertaken by the Department in January, 1954. Prior thereto the Commission successfully had negotiated for funds under Dingell-Johnson Project F3R for partial financing of the study.

The rockfish investigation, instituted in 1954, is one of the most important ever pursued by any conservation agency. Of all Maryland's finfish, from the standpoint of the commercial as well as the sports fishery, the rock (striped bass) is by far the most valuable. The information and data already assembled relative to the rock: the areas and times of spawning, success of spawning, the migratory behavior of the fish and the value of existing law protecting the brood stock are of incalculable assistance to management. They will become even more so as the study continues to progress.

PUBLIC RELATIONS

In public relations the Department's effort is centered on press releases, public speaking by staff members, exhibits and correspondence with and distribution of informative literature to the general public. Press releases are issued only when there exists factual information and data worthy of being conveyed to the public. Members of the Department's staff speak at dinner meetings of fraternal and other civic organizations. The subject material of exhibits, depicting the activities of the Department, has been expanded and improved. Correspondence with the public runs from simple requests for literature to letters necessitating lengthy and technical replies. It totals thousands of letters and post cards each year.

SUPPLY, MAINTENANCE AND REPAIR

In April of 1956 the Commission created, within the Department, a Supply Division with complete warehousing facilities for the storage and issue of materials and supplies having a recurring demand, particularly in connection with the maintenance, repair and operation of patrol craft.

The Maintenance and Repair Division, established at the Matapeake Terminal, Kent Island in 1954, is the headquarters for the maintenance and repair of the forty-three boats in the Department's patrol fleet. Tremendous savings have been made by this Division especially in exercising preventive maintenance.

Department of Game and Inland Fish

The Department of Game and Inland Fish is under the legal control of a five-man, unpaid commission appointed by the Governor. Commission members serve for staggered terms of five years each, so that only one appointment or reappointment is made each year. The commission elects its own chairman annually in July. The commission is legally responsible for the administrative policies of the Department and is authorized to make rules and regulations which supplement laws relating to game and fresh-water fish passed by the General Assembly.

Most farms have areas which are unsuited to cultivation but which are productive of vegetation which will provide food, shelter and nesting sites for wildlife. More than 550 farmers throughout the State have entered into agreement with the Department to devote tracts of this kind to wildlife. These tracts, averaging 12 acres each, are closed to hunting and become islands of safety for wildlife native to these areas. The Department supplies seed or seedlings which will provide food and shelter for birds and animals and the farmer agrees to maintain the area as a wildlife sanctuary. As game increases on these areas, it overflows into the surrounding fields and woods.

Though game birds and game animals belong to the public, most of the land on which these species are found is owned by private individuals. Therefore, the hunter may find himself provided with a license but have no place where he may hunt. In recent years the Department has purchased 30,502 acres of land in 29 tracts located in 15 counties. Some of these areas are marshlands suitable for waterfowl, muskrat and shore birds. Other tracts are located in forest areas in the Piedmont region or in the mountainous territory of western Maryland where deer, grouse and wild turkeys find an ideal habitat. Of this State-owned land, 18,801 acres in 12 separate tracts are open to licensed hunters. The State now owns approximately 150,000 acres in State forests which are likewise public hunting grounds.

Of the 30,502 acres purchased by the Department, 25 tracts containing 11,164 acres have been closed to hunting and have been developed as permanent game sanctuaries to supplement the system of refuges maintained by farmers.

FISH IN NON-TIDAL WATERS

Most streams of Maryland reach a summer temperature of 70° Fahrenheit or higher. Trout cannot thrive at such temperatures, and naturally such streams cannot support permanent breeding populations of trout. Nevertheless, excellent trout fishing is available throughout much of the State. The Department of Game and Inland Fish operates a number of hatcheries and rearing pools which have abundant supplies of clear, cold water throughout the year. Trout reared to legal size in these hatcheries and rearing stations can readily be transplanted to our lakes and streams. They feed, thrive, grow and provide excellent trout fishing until streams become warm in midsummer. Some streams in western Maryland, of course, support trout throughout the year.

Maryland is thus able to satisfy thousands of enthusiastic trout fishermen who would otherwise be compelled to forgo this sport or to spend their recreation funds in nearby states where hatchery trout are available.

Smallmouth bass, largemouth bass, bluegills, crappie, yellow perch and similar warm-water fish are less exacting than trout in their requirements. All of these and many more species readily breed in non-tidal waters throughout the State. Fishermen increase in numbers annually but the hook-and-line is an old, old device and is unlikely to seriously deplete a vigorous population of fish. During the present administration the Department of Game and Inland Fish has found it possible and even advisable to relax further and further a number of former restrictions on fishing in non-tidal waters.

These warm-water fish flourish throughout the State, but waters accessible to the fishermen have hitherto been limited. Formerly the fisherman found himself provided with tackle and a license but no suitable place in which to fish. The Department is rapidly providing a solution for this problem. In the past eight years the Department has built or purchased for public use 24 ponds and lakes throughout the State. These are generally referred to as community ponds. Each is surrounded by a margin of land provided with picnic facilities and landscaped in a simple manner. Each pond is stocked with appropriate species of warm-water fish and each is accessible to anyone licensed to fish in non-tidal waters.

Since World War II landowners throughout the country have shown a growing interest in the construction of the small impoundments usually referred to as farm ponds. Landowners and farmers in Maryland have shared this interest and during the years, 1950 to 1957, 1,561 farm ponds are known to have been built in Maryland. Such ponds are built primarily as a water supply for livestock and fire control. These ponds also provide an ideal habitat for warm-water fish, and the Department supplies bass and bluegills for stocking most of these ponds.

SUMMARY OF PROGRESS

In the year ending June 30, 1950 the State of Maryland sold 120,461 hunters' licenses and 73,128 anglers' licenses. In the year ending June 30, 1958 there were 165,699 licensed hunters and 100,596 licensed anglers. The growth in hunters and fishermen under the present administration was therefore about 40 percent. How has wildlife fared during this period?

During the past eight years the Department has constructed and opened to the public 24 community lakes and ponds, has improved and extended its trout rearing facilities and has stocked literally hundreds of farm ponds. Farmers have established more than 550 farm game propagation areas and the Department has purchased and improved 18,812 acres of public hunting grounds and 11,701 acres of State game refuges.

In the 1950 hunting season 890 deer were killed in 6 counties; in 1957 hunters took about 4,000 deer in 18 counties. Beaver have returned to the State, are well established at several points, and we may soon again be able to sell beaver pelts as we did in the seventeenth century. Wild turkeys appear to be flourishing, particularly in Worcester County and in the mountains of western Maryland. The grouse range is limited in Maryland but this species appears to be maintaining itself with no diminution in numbers or distribution. Raccoons have increased in recent years and are abundant throughout the State. Rabbits, squirrels and other small game are common and the Department receives more annoyance complaints against the prevalence of these small game animals than against their scarcity.

License fees paid by Maryland hunters and fishermen form the sole support of the Department of Game and Inland Fish; no general tax revenues whatever are expended on wildlife resources. A recent nationwide survey indicates that individual hunters and fishermen spend annually $71 and $70, respectively, on food, lodging, travel and other services which contribute to the general prosperity. Though hunters and fishermen increase annually in numbers, many of our game and freshwater fish are increasing at an equal or greater rate, and Maryland hunters and fishermen at this point have more and better opportunities for recreation than at any similar time within the last century.

Department of Research and Education

The Department of Research and Education, with headquarters at the Chesapeake Biological Laboratory in Calvert County, has provided an increasing flow of valuable research and scientific information about oysters, crabs, fish, forests, wildlife and other natural resources of the State. It also has served as a unique educational center in providing students and citizens of the State with knowledge and understanding about our fundamentally important resources. The scientific staff of the Department has served State officials, legislators and other public and private groups concerned with the protection and wise utilization of resources.

CHESAPEAKE BIOLOGICAL LABORATORY

The Chesapeake Biological Laboratory, which has the distinction of being the oldest State-supported research laboratory in the eastern United States, has been enlarged and new facilities have been added. Since oysters and the new soft clam industry provide the most valuable of our commercial Bay resources, these have received maximum attention.

The Laboratory now has established the pattern of oyster setting for all major areas of the Bay and its tributaries as a guide to efficient management efforts. New seed oysters from other States have been tested to determine their value in Maryland.

An entirely new soft clam industry has come into existence in Maryland since 1951 and expanded a million dollar annual yield. It brought grave problems and marvelous possibilities. The Chesapeake Biological Laboratory conducted an exhaustive survey of the soft shell clam that has been widely used by watermen and legislators.

This competent and impartial research by the Laboratory has aided the expansion of this industry and simultaneously assured reasonable protection for the older established resources. Of practical value to all users of the Bay is the knowledge derived from the Laboratory's studies of where and when shipworms enter unprotected wooden structures.

FISHERIES RESEARCH

Fisheries research has further illuminated the life history, early developmental stages and migratory habits of Maryland's rockfish or striped bass. A thorough study was made of the white perch, which is also one of the most important commercial and sports species.

For the first time, effective creel censuses have been made of some of the sports fisheries of the Chesapeake Bay fishing areas and these, with the efficient commercial catch record system already developed by the Department, form an invaluable reference and necessary guide for managing Bay species. Cooperative studies with the U. S. Navy on the effects of underwater explosives on Bay marine fish have indicated that the damage is temporary and local. Areas of least probable damage from explosives to rockfish have been designated by the Department and adopted by the Navy for future work.

The old problems of the Conowingo Dam area have been attacked through a new and imaginative approach to a thorough investigation of the need for passage of fish. The study is supported by a three-year contract between this Department and the Susquehanna Electric Company and supervised by an Advisory Committee containing some of the outstanding fishery biologists of the world.

In Chincoteague Bay effective progress has been made to insure and enlarge the future supply of the delectable Chincoteague oyster. New ways of producing seed have been developed and tested, and a cooperative program is underway with the U. S. Fish and Wildlife Service for studying methods to control the dreaded oyster drills of the area. The hard shell clam producing bottoms have been charted and interpreted to understand which environmental factors affect the clam crop.

CRAB SUPPLY STUDIED

New methods of predicting the crab supply are under test. These may remove the economic losses which have resulted from rapid and unexpected fluctuations. A bibliography of all the literature in the world dealing with the Maryland type of crab has been published.

New research studies of the biology of the troublesome jellyfish have been undertaken which may provide clues leading to eventual control of this organism.

CHESAPEAKE BAY INSTITUTE

The Department was instrumental in the creation of the Chesapeake Bay Institute of The Johns Hopkins University, which conducts research on the chemistry and physics of the Bay and its tributaries. This Institute has solved some of the pressing practical problems of the Bay area and achieved high international reputation through its work on the basic problems of this estuary.

MARYLAND WEATHER SERVICE

The Maryland Weather Service supplements the operation of the U. S. Weather Bureau at the Friendship International Airport. The Service has produced special assistance on local Maryland problems and aided in the protection of fruit crops, proper location of new industries and other problems related to weather and climate.

INLAND RESOURCES DIVISION

The Inland Resources Division has fully surveyed the fresh waters and forests of the State so that accurate knowledge is, for the first time, available on the quantity and quality of these resources in each County. Broad, original research projects have been initiated that are designed to improve woodland utilization and the fresh water fishing and hunting which provide recreation for Maryland citizens.

Studies concerning the gray squirrel have resulted in a more appropriate hunting season for this animal, preventing the destruction of nursing females and saving vast numbers of baby squirrels. These, like most projects of this Department, are made possible and efficient by close co-operation with other State and federal departments and agencies.

CONSERVATION EDUCATION

In the field of Conservation Education, an imaginative teachers' workshop has been created. School teachers of Maryland now can participate in one of the best presentations in this country of information and inspiration about natural resources. Teachers have carried back into their classrooms in every County and Baltimore City the concepts of conservation as they apply to the highly varied problems of the "Old Line State."

Expert consultant service in conservation education has been provided to the Maryland Department of Education, to County school systems and to youth and civic groups. Many thousands of colored slides, pamphlets, teaching kits and other aids to teachers and students have been produced by the Department.

RESEARCH FACILITIES

To provide even greater research yield in the future, new research laboratory and storage facilities are under construction at Solomons. The research building, equipped with an excellent running salt water system, constant temperature room and other modern laboratory facilities will provide one of the best centers on the Atlantic Coast for research on estuarine animals and plants.

Addition of a research vessel provides a tool for more thorough study of Maryland's oyster beds and other bottoms, extensive collection of crabs and the most thorough sampling of fish ever undertaken in the Chesapeake Bay.

Department of Geology, Mines and Water Resources

The Department of Geology, Mines and Water Resources is a consolidation of the former Geological and Economic Survey established in 1896, the Water Front Commission established in 1929, and the Water Resources Commission established in 1933. Its major functions are: (1) topographic and geological surveys, (2) investigation of mineral and water resources, (3) control over use of surface and underground waters and construction of dams and reservoirs, and (4) protection of shore fronts and waterways against erosion. The consolidation was effected in 1941.

During the past eight years its activities in these fields have been greatly expanded and the scope of its responsibilities in them greatly increased by new legislation in conformity with growing interest and awareness of the people of Maryland of the fundamental importance of these natural resources in their immediate and future welfare.

GEOLOGICAL AND TOPOGRAPHIC MAPS

One of the most widely useful and used services of the Department is the provision of adequate county topographic maps. A completely new series of maps of the twenty-three counties was completed in 1956. To keep these maps up-to-date with the rapid growth of communities and the many new housing developments and the continuous expansion and growth of the road system, during the period, all of these maps have undergone revised printings, six of the counties two revisions, six of the counties three revisions, and one county five revisions. There were forty-five printings aggregating 98,000 maps.

Though charged against the annual budgets of the Department, the receipts from sales revert to the General Treasury. The increasing demand for these maps is reflected in the increasing percentage of the budget returned from sales, amounting to 6.2 percent in 1951 and 14 percent in 1957, despite the fact that the Department has managed to carry on increasing activities and augmented responsibilities with decreasing budgets. The average of the annual budget of the Department during the period is $103,600, but the expenditures in fiscal 1957 were $93,058, of which $11,522 was returned in sales and $1,510 in well driller license fees, making net expenditures of the Department only $80,026.

New geologic maps of Allegany, Garrett, Montgomery and Prince George's Counties were published, making large scale geologic maps available for all of the counties except for the five southernmost counties of the Eastern Shore in which the areal geology is so uniform that the State geologic map is adequate.

MINERAL RESOURCES

Clays are one of the State's most important and abundant mineral resources, yet little of the essential information regarding their mineralogic composition and ceramic properties was available. This lack was filled in part by an investigation of the refractory clays of the Maryland Coal Measures. The important clays of the Coastal Plain extending across Cecil, Harford, Baltimore, Anne Arundel and Prince George's Counties are being studied with respect to the mineralogic and ceramic properties that determine their suitability for various industrial uses.

Development of the Mt. Lake Park gas field was closely followed by the Department and in 1954 a large scale structure map of the field was published. To forestall the inevitable wasteful development that would result from exploitation of this field under the outmoded "law of capture," the Department pleaded in vain in 1951 for the enactment of proper conservation legislation.

However, in 1955 the Department succeeded in having reasonably sound oil and gas conservation legislation enacted.

Upon recommendation of the Department, the U. S. Bureau of Mines had carried out extensive exploratory programs of core drilling in the Georges Creek, Upper Potomac, and Castleman Coal Basins, the results of which yielded valuable information on the quality of the lesser developed coal seams and on the magnitude of their coal reserves.

The report on the Castleman Basin published in 1952 estimated the reserves in seams over 28 inches thick at 80,000,000 tons and in seams over 14 inches thick at 232,000,000 tons. In another report on these explorations in 1953 the reserves of coking coal in Allegany County in seams over 28 inches thick were estimated at over 304,000,000 tons. These explorations demonstrated that the reserves in the lower seams in these coal basins can compensate for the approaching exhaustion of the Big Vein and sustain the Maryland coal industry for many years.

WATER RESOURCES

The major project of the Department has been the compilation of a complete inventory of all the available water resources throughout the state.

Ninety stream flow measuring stations, distributed throughout the State geographically and by type of streams, were operated. The flow of data are being analyzed for flood flow and low flow frequency to determine the conditions under which the surface waters of the State are available with respect to time and volume.

The salinity ranges along the courses of the principal rivers of the Eastern Shore were determined to outline the areas in which these surface waters may be safely used for irrigation.

The ground waters have been inventoried county by county. During the period the results of these investigations were published covering seventeen counties and the results in two other counties are awaiting publication. The investigations in the last two counties are well under way. In addition the results of an intensive study of the ground-water resources of the Baltimore Industrial Area and a comprehensive summary of the ground-water resources of the five Southern Maryland Counties were published.

In the discharge of its responsibilities in water resources, during the first seven years of the period, the Department made periodic measurements of fluctuations in water levels in several hundred observation wells geographically distributed throughout the State, issued more than 21,000 permits to drill wells, issued over 700 permits to use and appropriate ground water aggregating an allowance of over 27,000,000 gallons of water a day, and approved nearly 1,600 farm ponds.

No other State has as complete an inventory of its water resources, and especially of its ground-water resources. The inventory has established that Maryland is now using only 6 percent of the annual rate of replenishment of its water resources. It has disproven the still often repeated erroneous assertions that water levels are declining in Maryland and that there is imminent danger of a shortage of water resources.

The Maryland policy governing the use of its water resources, enacted in 1933, has been eminently satisfactory and successful and is widely recognized as the soundest legislation that has been enacted in any of the humid States. The phrasing of the 1933 law inadvertently excluded from control under that policy the then unforeseen use of water for supplemental irrigation. The inevitable need to remedy this recently developed flaw in the law has been urged by the Department since 1955, in which it has had the support of Governor McKeldin.

SHORE EROSION PROTECTION

A survey of the amount of erosion along Maryland's tidewater shores during a period of ninety years showed an average annual loss of 3,300 acres. Wherever requested, the Department has investigated erosion conditions and recommended remedial measures for protection. During the years 1951 to 1957, 120 such investigations were made.

A closely related function of the Department is to review reports of the Corps of Engineers, United States Army, on proposed river and harbor improvements, and to supplement them with a statement of the State's interest in the projects. During the period 1951 to 1957, fourteen reports were reviewed. It has long been recognized by the Department that many proposed minor river and harbor improvements for which the expectable general navigation benefits are inadequate to qualify them for solely Federal aid, have significant expectable local benefits to the State, the county, and to the residents of the waterway that warrant State or intra-State financial aid, but its repeated recommendations that such legislation be enacted have not been carried out.

An important contribution to the problem of siltation of the tidal waters of the State was made by an investigation of siltation in the Chesapeake Bay, the results of which were published in 1953.

MISCELLANEOUS

Of very general interest and usefulness are Bulletin 19, "Geography and Geology of Maryland," published in 1956, and Bulletin 20, "Miocene Fossils of Maryland," published in 1957.

There had long been a demand, both public and in the schools, for an account of the economic and physical geography and the geology and mineral resources of Maryland written for such readers rather than for the professional scientist. Bulletin 19 supplied that need.

BUREAU OF MINES

The principal function of this Bureau is to inspect coal and fire clay mines with the objective of reducing the number of mine accidents and increasing the efficiency and economy of mining.

To further insure the safety of those employed in the coal mining industry, the Bureau maintains a mobile rescue truck which is available at all times for any emergency not only in coal mines but any disaster which might occur.

Since January, 1951, money has been appropriated in the budget each year for the purchase of modern equipment. Some of the items purchased were a High Pressure Oxygen Pump, a Pneolator, 5-Oxygen Breathing Apparatus, Gas Masks, etc.

In 1954, through the efforts of the Bureau, a Civil Defense Building was erected in Kitzmiller, Maryland, and the Department's rescue truck and equipment are housed in a fire-proof room in this building.

In conjunction with mine safety, the Bureau maintains a Mine Rescue Team which is trained in all phases of rescue work. To January 31, 1958, a total of 47 men have been trained. The Rescue Team, in October, 1951 at the National Mine Rescue Contest in Columbus, Ohio, outclassed its closest competition by a margin of 12 minutes. Since January, 1951, the Rescue Team has had 102 training sessions.

During the past seven years, the mine inspectors have trained a total of 360 persons in first aid. In addition to coal miners, this includes local industries, police and fire departments, Boy Scouts and Girl Scouts.

The Bureau of Mines cooperates with the Maryland Civil Defense Agency in providing this rescue and first aid training.

Since 1923, the Bureau of Mines has been conducting an educational program in coal mining, etc., in cooperation with the University of Maryland and the State Department of Education for Allegany and Garrett Counties. In September, 1955, when the University of Maryland and the State Department of Education discontinued sponsorship of this program, this department took over complete responsibility for teaching these classes. The District Mine Inspectors conduct these classes in addition to their regular duties. Since 1951, the total enrollment has been 819. The purpose of this program is to prepare persons for First Class Mine Foreman Certificates.

It is the general opinion that this educational program has been the main factor in minimizing mine fatalities in Maryland as there have been no mine fatalities since 1953.

LABORATORY SET UP

In 1951, a laboratory was established in the office of the Bureau of Mines for the purpose of making coal analyses. In the beginning, the laboratory was only equipped to determine quantitative amounts of ash, moisture, volatile combustible matter and fixed carbon in coal. With the addition of new equipment each year, the laboratory is now equipped to make a complete proximate analysis of coal. In 1956, a Gas Analysis Apparatus was added to the laboratory facilities. The main purpose of this apparatus is to determine the presence of methane in mine atmospheres.

The laboratory is maintained by an employee of this department known as the Fuel Combustion Adviser. Upon his advice both on quality and preparation of coal at the mine and by advising consumers as to proper combustion practices, the quality of Maryland coal has improved. The State Purchasing Department has used this program to a great extent both to improve the quality of coal purchased and to obtain a greater degree of efficiency in burning coal at State Institutions.

On June 1, 1955, the Maryland Strip Mining Laws went into effect. This law provides for the reclamation of land damaged by strip mining. To January 21, 1958, thirty-nine Permits have been issued to coal operators by this department. Of this number, eight have been completed to the satisfaction of this Bureau. After this law went into effect, it was necessary for our mine inspectors to keep a close check on all strip operations measuring acreage, etc. and to see that all sections of the laws were being complied with. In July, 1957, funds were appropriated for the purchase of three Jeeps to facilitate the inspection of these operations.

The Bureau of Mines plays an important part in the economy of the State of Maryland. From January 1, 1951 through December 31, 1957, 4,039,060 tons of coal were produced within the State at an average market price of $5.00 per ton, or $20,195,300. During this same period 566,627 tons of fire clay were produced.

There are approximately 1.5 billion tons of recoverable coal reserves in Western Maryland. Due to the number of inquiries this department has received during the past several years, it is evident that there is an increased interest in these reserves.

It is the general opinion that the future of the coal industry in Maryland continues to be very optimistic.

Water Pollution Control Commission

The maintenance of the waters of Maryland in a wholesome condition through the abatement and control of pollution is a necessary function of government. To carry out this function the Water Pollution Control Commission was created in 1947 by the General Assembly of Maryland.

Commission policy and program have progressed from action in 1947 to prohibit gross pollution of State waters to more recent action constituting a more complex and diversified attack on all aspects of the problem. In 1952 the Commission applied stricter controls on discharges from food-processing and food-packing plants.

In the same year, the Certificate of Approval regulation was issued which requires assurance that no water pollution problem will result before approval is granted for any project. In 1955, the Commission adopted a special regulation for the Baltimore Harbor area carefully designed to fit the needs and uses of this water region.

CONTROL PROGRAM

The regulations promulgated by the Commission have been carefully fashioned so as to be both practical and effective, so as to be not only technically attainable but also financially feasible, also as not to impose upon the State's industrial and municipal economy an expense which is out of proportion to the benefits sought.

In order to prohibit gross impairment of State waters, the Commission promulgated in 1947, Regulation I, which makes unlawful discharge of oil, and Regulation II, which makes unlawful the discharge of garbage and food containers.

There can be no quarrel with the plain and straightforward warning embodied in Regulations I and II that the State will not tolerate the wanton despoilment of its waters by such noxious materials as oil and garbage.

REGULATIONS REVISED

On June 6, 1952, the Water Pollution Control Commission took a decisive step toward improved pollution control by withdrawing its Regulation III, which established minimal standards for food-processing and packing plants in Maryland, and made Regulation IV applicable to all industries.

The specific purpose of Regulation IV is the control of water pollution caused by the wastes from industrial establishments. Primarily, Regulation IV may be termed an effluent standard, that is to say, the condition of the effluent is controlled before entering State waters.

In 1948, when Regulation IV was first issued, the Commission felt that an "effluent standard"-type regulation would, at that time, serve best the interests of the people. Experience during the ensuing years has demonstrated that this regulation is a useful tool for water pollution control.

The numerical limits specified in Regulation IV with adjustment for the out-of-the-ordinary situation as permitted by the regulation, will normally differentiate between satisfactory and unsatisfactory discharges to the waters of the State.

Since its inception, Regulation IV has been amended and adjusted five times, whenever the attention of the Commission was directed to a way in which the existing regulation might be improved.

An active and effective water pollution control program must have as its foundation reliable up-to-date data and information. This need was recognized in 1952 when the Commission approved Regulation V which requires the submission of reports for the discharge of industrial waste and for the issuance of certificates of approval for the construction and alteration of industrial waste treatment works.

Since May, 1952, a total of one hundred thirteen cerificates of approval have been issued for waste treatment projects of varying scope; each and every certificate of approval represents another step forward in the fight against pollution.

MAJOR DECISION

Yet another major decision in the field of water pollution control in Maryland was made by the Commission on December 14, 1955, when it approved and adopted its Regulation IV-A which establishes reasonable receiving water quality standards as well as general effluent characteristics for the Baltimore Harbor area. Regulation IV-A represents a painstaking, considered effort by the Commission to provide a control standard to fit the special requirements of this area. Regulation IV-A represents the result of the most comprehensive study made of the Baltimore Harbor to date. This study concluded that:

1. "In order of economic importance, the primary uses of water in Baltimore Harbor are for navigation, waste disposal, industrial water supply and recreation.
2. "The Patapsco Estuary appears to have the ability to assimilate much greater loads of organic matter and acid than are being discharged at present. Degraded conditions are occasioned in limited peripheral areas by imposition of waste loads in excess of local assimilative capacities.
3. "Existing conditions can be improved by transferring pollution loads from peripheral areas of limited assimilative capacities to the principal fairway, or by abating local waste discharges.
4. "There is no indication that waste disposal as normally practiced in the area has any significant effect on water quality in Chesapeake Bay outside Baltimore Harbor."

It is believed that these regulations make possible in the waters of the State the practical enforcement of the provisions and intent of the Water Pollution Control Law of Maryland.

REVIEW OF ACTIVITIES

In review, the following activities and accomplishments of the Water Pollution Control Commission deserve special mention:

1. Changes in regulations and the adoption of new regulations which have resulted in decided improvements in the pollution control program.

2. The establishment of a modern, up-to-date analytical laboratory to serve the Commission in the effective control of water pollution in Maryland.
3. An enlarged staff and increased budget which has made possible stricter surveillance and more rigid enforcement of pollution control measures.
4. A policy of reasonable yet vigorous control which has fostered a cooperative spirit among Maryland's industries, and which will continue to yield substantial benefits in improved water quality.

It is realized, of course, that many water pollution problems still exist and that much remains to be done. The Commission intends to continue an all-out effort to bring water pollution in Maryland under complete control.

Soil Conservation Committee

The 1937 session of the Maryland General Assembly established the State Soil Conservation Committee under the State Board of Agriculture. This enabling legislation authorized the formation of local soil conservation districts. The State Soil Conservation Committee was given the job of helping with the formation of districts wherever the local people request such assistance. By law, it is responsible for offering such help as is possible and practical to the supervisors of soil conservation districts in carrying out their local programs. It keeps the supervisors of each district informed of activities and experiences in other districts and links their problems in a common cause when this is possible and is requested by the districts.

The committee also helps districts secure the help and advice of state and federal agencies who have resources which can be brought to bear on soil and water problems. It further is charged with keeping the people of Maryland informed about the work of soil conservation districts.

MAJOR ACCOMPLISHMENTS

During this seven-year period the number of farms with conservation farm plans has increased from 9,696 to 16,271. These farm plans include a variety of conservation practices for the control of erosion and conservation of water. Good conservation farm planning represents an effort to treat every acre of farm land according to its needs and use it within its capabilities. In order to accomplish this objective, major land use changes are an important part of the program. Some of the major accomplishments, including farm practices, which have been applied to farm land in accordance with the conservation plans are listed below indicating the amount of each practice applied during the past seven years:

Soil Surveys completed (acres)	983,000
Conservation farm plans (number)	6,575
Contour cultivation (acres)	79,000
Contour strip cropping (acres)	59,000
Pasture improvement (acres)	126,000
Farm ponds constructed (number)	1,936
Drainage systems (acres)	78,000
Sprinkler irrigation systems (number)	191

STORAGE OF WATER IN FARM PONDS

The State Soil Conservation Committee has worked closely with farm groups in the State in helping to formulate legislation which would make it possible to store more water in the farm ponds for irrigation, stock water, fire protection and recreation. As a result of these efforts, farm ponds now may be constructed as large as five acres in surface area and 15 feet in depth, providing the drainage area does not exceed 400 acres in the Piedmont and mountain sections of the State, and 700 acres in the coastal plain. An amendment to Article 66(c) of the Maryland Code places the responsibility for approval of plans and supervision of construction on the State Soil Conservation Committee. Plans and specifications, as well as construction notices, still must be filed with the Department of Geology, Mines and Water Resources for review.

WATERSHED PROTECTION AND FLOOD PREVENTION

Governor McKeldin designated the State Board of Agriculture as the approving agency for watershed applications submitted under Public Law 566. The State Board of Agriculture in turn delegated this responsibility to the State Soil Conservation Committee. The State Soil Conservation Committee has assisted 13 watershed associations with their organizational problems and has approved ten applications for planning assistance. Three of these applications have been approved by the federal government for construction. Three more are expected to receive federal approval in the near future. Construction is under way in the Little Deer Creek watershed in Harford County. Only 69 have been approved for the entire country.

Inasmuch as land treatment is an important requirement in the program being carried out under the Watershed Protection and Flood Prevention Act, the program has resulted in getting more conservation established on the land in these watersheds.

The Maryland-National Capital Park and Planning Commission

The seven year period ending January 1, 1958 was one of massive change for The Maryland-National Capital Park and Planning Commission.

Some of the highlights of this seven year period include:

Creation of an Advance Planning Section which was to draft a comprehensive General Plan as a guide for the orderly physical development of the region.

Enlargement of the Commission's area of planning jurisdiction, the Maryland-Washington Regional District, from 283 square miles to 691 square miles; and the area of park jurisdiction, the Maryland-Washington Metropolitan District, from 188 to 203 square miles.

Addition of 1,659 acres of new parklands to its park system at a cost of $2,639,564.

Development of park facilities at a cost of $1,939,691.

Approval of more than 2,000 subdivision plats, clearing the way for development of thousands of acres of new homes, shopping centers and roadways.

These were years of crisis for the Park and Planning Commission in its role of guiding the physical growth of the region. Population increased 73 per cent in the Regional District, rising from 315,000 to 542,000 during the seven year span.

The phenomenon which has become known as "urban sprawl" was an ever-present danger, threatening to engulf the invitingly green fields and woodlands of the Maryland Counties adjoining the Nation's Capital.

Land speculators and developers, eager to reap the profits assured through mass production of housing, leap-frogged each other in constant search of cheaper land. With each leap, the limits of suburbia reached deeper into the green countryside.

A factor seriously hampering the ability of the Commission to control, contain and channel this new growth was the limitation of time. The staff of the Commission was constantly wrestling with the problems generated daily and was unable to devote itself to the larger task of looking ahead six weeks, six months or six years.

NEW ADVANCE PLANNING SECTION

The Commission met this challenge in January, 1954, by creation of its Advance Planning Section. The staff of this new section immediately began the first phase of work toward development of a general plan, a land use survey.

The land use survey was a necessary starting point since it would be impossible to plan for the future without precise knowledge of existing conditions. This survey entailed hundreds of hours of field work to determine the actual uses to which the land of the region was being put.

Population density figures, based upon types of housing, were by-products of these studies. With this information, it was possible to begin work on other elements of the general plan, such as plotting the most desirable locations for schools, parks, shopping centers, industrial areas, highways and other public facilities.

The land use survey was completed in two years. The information was published and distributed to the general public in late 1955.

Seven technical bulletins were prepared during this period and widespread distribution of the information was achieved. This distribution had the dual functions of acquainting the public with existing conditions and the need for a carefully devised general plan.

MASTER HIGHWAY PLAN

One of the earliest detailed plans of the Commission was its Master Plan of Highways, adopted in May, 1953. With the wealth of new information available as a result of these detailed studies, it was possible to revise the highway plan in June, 1955.

Such major highway projects as the Washington Circumferential Highway which will provide a 36-mile stretch of road through Montgomery and Prince George's Counties as a by-pass route for traffic seeking to avoid congested metropolitan streets were evolved in this highway plan. The first portion of the roadway has already been constructed.

Another recommendation of the highway plan has won the approval of the State Roads Commission. It is the proposed Northern Parkway. This would become a major radial route within the suburban Maryland area as well as a direct link between the District of Columbia, Baltimore and Gettysburg.

By mid-1955, sufficient data had been gathered to begin preparation of a Master Plan of Schools, Parks and Recreation. This plan is an essential element of the general plan since it indicates where and, to some extent, when additional school and park sites will be needed to serve the expanding population. This plan was adopted in July, 1956 after extensive public hearings.

The final step was the correlation of the data which had been gathered. This resulted in adoption of the comprehensive General Plan in November, 1957. This document is the guide for the future location of subdivisions, commercial areas, industrial centers, schools, parks, highways and other public facilities through the year 1980.

SUBDIVISION CONTROL

Through judicious exercise of subdivision control authority, the Commission has already played an important role in shaping and balancing the land use pattern of the region. It has also saved hundreds of thousands of tax dollars by the reservation and dedication rights which are part of subdivision control.

In reviewing subdivision plans, the Commission carefully considers the need in a given area for school, highway or other public uses. If the need is evident, the Commission forestalls development on the particular tracts involved through the reservation authority. In some cases outright dedication is achieved resulting in no acquisition cost to the agency needing the land.

In zoning matters, the Commission plays the role of advisor to the two governing bodies, helping to shape the final decisions that effect implementation of the General Plan.

Through its park function, the Commission has further implemented the General Plan, purchasing parklands in areas indicated on the plan to help provide a harmonious balance between open areas and built-up developments.

PARK-SCHOOL JOINT PROGRAM

One of the major achievements of the Park Department of the Commission has been to spearhead the concept of cooperation between park and school authorities in the acquisition of land. This has resulted in increasing emphasis on the joint purchase of property at savings to each agency and, ultimately, the taxpayers.

Under the park-school joint acquisition program, the Commission provides the play facilities needed for the school program on land immediately adjacent to the school building. This reduces the total land needs since each agency shares some of the facilities provided by the other. It also prevents duplication of similar facilities by the two agencies in local neighborhoods.

During the past seven years, the Commission has provided more than 100 athletic fields and more than 200 picnic areas in its parklands. In addition, 25 community center buildings have been erected, providing facilities for scout groups and other local organizations to conduct their activities in park settings.

Five miles of park roads have been added to the Commission's road network, providing access to the facilities in the 4,300 acre park system.

The Department of Information

Although launched as an agency in 1949, the Department of Information first was given full departmental status in 1951.

It concentrates on the attraction of tourists to Maryland and the promotion of travel in the State.

In 1951, it was producing nine publications of tourist and travel interest.

By 1957, the number of such printed publications had risen to 22 plus 75 items of tourist interest in mimeographed form.

In 1951, only 8,385 requests were received for printed information. The Department responded with 13,406 pieces of its literature.

In 1957, the requests totaled 65,665, and more than half a million copies were distributed.

There are many evidences of the effectiveness of the Department's activities.

Visitors to historic Annapolis, for example, have increased at a rapid rate, as indicated by the official registrations in the guest books at the State House.

In 1951, only 11,232 such visitors were recorded. In 1957, nearly 70,000 signed their names in the books.

Prior to 1951, the Deep Creek Lake area of Western Maryland was catering only to a small number of summer vacationists for a season of 12 weeks each year.

WINTER SPORTS PROMOTIONS

Organization of the Deep Creek Lake Promotion Council, on the urging and with the cooperation of the Department in 1951, and the institution of the Autumn Glory Festival as an annual event, has so changed the picture that Deep Creek Lake and its environs are rapidly winning national recognition as a year-around resort. In the winter, the only ski-run south of the Mason-Dixon Line attracts thousands of visitors.

Hunting and fishing activities have increased and a summer theater plays to capacity audiences. New motels, restaurants and other tourist accommodations have been opened or are being planned.

In 1956, the Department gave its concentrated treatment to St. Mary's County, Maryland's birthplace. At its urging, a St. Mary's County Devel-

Beach at Ocean City, preserved by macadam groins built by Roads Commission.

opment Committee was organized. The Department assisted in the preparation of publicity. The tourist business in the area is expanding rapidly with several new hostelries, marinas and other vacation facilities established and planned.

The Department assisted the commercial establishments along Route 40 in recovering much of the business that was lost when new turnpikes began carrying tourists rapidly through the area. The U. S. Route 40 Association was formed; attractive signs directed motorists to the accommodations, historic attractions and scenic beauty of old Forty. The Department aids in the distribution of the Route 40 folder.

Probably the first national convention housed entirely in motels resulted from the Department's suggestion to the operators of the fine establishments along Route 301 in Charles County that the American Forestry Association be invited to hold its annual meeting there in 1956. The devotion of an entire issue of American Forestry Magazine to the attractions of Maryland followed the event.

Similar assistance was provided for the business people along Route 1 when the new Baltimore-Washington Expressway attracted the great bulk of the traffic between the two cities. Strip maps, prepared by the Department, at the expense of the Route 1 Association, show Expressway motorists when they can obtain refreshments, rest, gasoline and sleeping accommodations on the nearby old Boulevard.

The Department works in close cooperation with the Ocean City Information Center in the successful promotion of Maryland's great seaside resort.

TRAVEL PARLEY

In 1954, at the suggestion of the Department, Governor McKeldin called a meeting of representatives of the Travel Vacation Industry. More than 400 persons attended the session in the State House, and the Maryland Travel Council was born.

Also in 1954, the Department sponsored a travel editors' tour of Maryland with some 40 writers from various parts of the United States and from Canada. The resultant publicity was so outstanding that the tour was repeated in 1955 and again in 1956. Various organizations and business establishments footed the bills.

In 1956, the Travel Council placed Maryland literature racks in various public places in New England. The racks were designed by the Department.

The Department began buying advertising space in national publications for the first time in 1957. The publications of the advertisements were followed by distribution of reprints in counter card form for display in places of public accommodation.

"Annapolis Index" is a weekly broadcast (WBAL) by the Director, dealing with Maryland history and modern travel opportunities. Recordings of some of the programs are used in the public schools.

In 1957, the Department enlisted the cooperation of Baltimore business people in producing an illustrated City map with text. More than 100,000 copies have been distributed.

The Department prepares Maryland material on request for encyclopedias and textbooks, and sometimes checks for authenticity such material written by others.

News releases, of course, are regularly sent out and pictures are furnished for all types of publications. Public speakers are accorded the full cooperation of the office in the preparation of talks on Maryland.

State Fair Board

With the support and guidance of the Fair Board, agricultural fairs and shows have steadily progressed. Now Maryland has a series of unsurpassed agricultural expositions. The fair and exhibit program in this State consists of twenty-seven fairs and shows, and seventy-eight community exhibits and field days in addition to our State Fair. Six hundred and forty-five thousand spectators attend these functions annually and thirty-five thousand five hundred exhibitors enter more than ninety-nine thousand exhibits each year.

Without the cooperation of this agency, the maintenance and improvement of the facilities of fairs, to accommodate increased exhibits and participation by exhibitors, would be impossible. In addition, the grants made by this agency enable fair managements to offer premiums worthy of the skill required of farm people to develop agricultural exhibits of the high quality that is necessary to meet the competition encountered in today's fairs.

Educational exhibits are becoming each year a more important phase of fairs and shows, particularly with regard to informing the consumer and the farmer of the technological advances in our agricultural industry. Emphasis is placed on the production and marketing of agricultural products. The trend of educational exhibits pointing out these important steps has been particularly significant since 1951 and will have even greater bearing on the planning for fairs and shows in the future.

From the one-day show at the community level up to our larger County fairs and then to our State Fair, the accomplishments of our farm people, adults and children, have been particularly outstanding.

LEARNING BY DOING

Learning by doing is a maxim of our rural youth. The opportunity to put this philosophy into practical use is provided by our fair program and the experience gained has made possible accomplishments by our young farmers and homemakers which have stood the test of time and considerably enhanced the efficiency and quality of our agricultural industry.

Particularly outstanding is the record of Maryland's 4-H dairy and livestock judging project. More than four hundred boys and girls receive instruction and training throughout the State on the County level, and a team of three is selected in each County to receive additional training and compete in the local contest usually held at a County fair. Final competition is held at the State Fair, and the winners are given advanced training preparatory to national competition.

Since 1951, this program, assisted by this agency, has resulted in Maryland's being first in the nation five times as well as first in international competition on two occasions. However, the most important result of such an outstanding record is the stimulating leadership which these people give after they have returned to their communities and passed on the benefits of their training and experience to those who are preparing to follow in their footsteps.

BOARD SUPPORT

Without the support and cooperation of this agency, the development of Maryland's program of agricultural fairs and exhibits would, in most instances, have been impossible. Nevertheless, the Maryland State Fair Board is keenly aware that much remains to be done to develop an ideal program. Furthermore, as conditions in Maryland agriculture change, a continuous process of innovation and adaptation must be carried on within the fair program.

Committee to Keep Maryland Beautiful

When Governor McKeldin, in 1954, appointed his Committee To Keep Maryland Beautiful, this State became the pioneer in the movement to establish State branches of the then recently formed Keep America Beautiful organization.

John E. Clark, Bel Air attorney, has headed the Maryland Committee since its inception. The Committee is composed at present of nearly 100 civic and business leaders throughout the State.

Keep Maryland Beautiful is a year-around program of education, emphasized by an annual Spring Clean-up Week proclaimed by the Governor for special projects of community beautification.

TRASH CONTAINERS

One of the most important contributions of our State program to Keep America Beautiful has been the Travel Trash container. With the cooperation of oil companies, service stations throughout the State are installing Travel Trash containers.

These containers are not only a convenience for the motorists, but serve as a constant reminder that trash belongs in a container. Travel Trash containers in service stations and the use of litterbags by motorists is proving the most effective answer to the highway litter problem. Other States are expanding this program.

The joint action of public agencies, civic organizations, community groups, newspapers, radio and TV throughout the State has achieved approximately a 25% decrease in litter along Maryland highways, in parks and on beaches. The complete elimination of litter, which will be achieved when each individual accepts his responsibility to properly dispose of his own trash, is the first goal.

However, roadside and community beautification projects already have been initiated; for an even more beautiful Maryland for all to appreciate and enjoy is the never-ending quest. As Governor McKeldin has said, "In organizing and maintaining this Keep Maryland Beautiful movement, we have started a job that never can be ended."

Maryland Racing Commission

The Maryland Racing Commission was created by the General Assembly in 1920. The jurisdiction and powers of the Commission extend to all persons, associations, and corporations which conduct any racing meetings within the State of Maryland where there is any stake, purse or reward offered. The Commission consists of three members appointed by the Governor of whom not more than two are of the same political party, and one of whom is designated by the Governor to be the Chairman.

During the past eight years there has been remarkable progress in

Maryland's traditional sport. Using financial statistics solely as an index of the progress of the sport, the consistent increase of public support to Maryland racing is impressive.

In 1951 revenue to the State from racing amounted to $5,460,477.09. One year later revenue had increased approximately $1,000,000.

By 1957 racing revenues had risen to a total of $9,148,906.84. Thus in a period of seven years the State's revenue from racing has risen approximately 67.5% or a total increase of $3,688,429.75. Gratifying as this increase in revenue may be, it is even more significant to those who seek to preserve the tradition of Maryland racing.

But revenue dollars are not the only measure of progress during the same eight-year period. Substantial capital expenditures were made at all of the major and minor flat tracks and at the harness tracks for the benefit of the patrons of racing. These improvements were all first submitted to the Racing Commission for review and approval before work was authorized in each case.

For example, Maryland State Fair built a new club house at Laurel, established the Turf Club and made extensive improvements in the grandstand area. This construction, in addition to modernizing the grandstand and building new barns and sleeping quarters for stable employees and enlarging parking facilities cost approximately $4,000,000.

BOWIE IMPROVEMENTS

A new racing strip was built at Bowie, a 77-stall receiving barn constructed, a new club house, dormitories and track kitchen were built as well as providing for the winter comfort of the patrons at the club house and in the betting area in the grandstand. These improvements cost the Southern Maryland Agricultural Association approximately $2,600,000.

At Pimlico the Maryland Jockey Club spent approximately $1,800,000 in building a new club house and making substantial improvements to the old club house. The Commission recognizes that local factors, including rapid urban development on all sides of Pimlico and zoning restrictions have, however, prevented realization of the potential which would otherwise have been expected at Pimlico.

In 1958 the Maryland State Fair and Agricultural Society completed its new grandstand at Timonium. Only two years before it had erected a new paddock, secretary's office and jockeys' quarters. The cost of all of these improvements at Timonium has been approximately $1,400,000.

Citing these instances of material progress at Maryland tracks is in no way tended to overlook the splendid work which has been done at Hagerstown, Marlboro and Bel Air, as well as at Rosecroft Raceway,

Laurel Raceway, and Baltimore Raceway with the guidance and approval of the Commission.

In performing its duty to regulate horse racing the Maryland Racing Commission has always kept foremost the object of continuing and promoting the great tradition of Maryland racing that has been a heritage from the earliest Colonial times.

Athletic Commission

The Maryland State Athletic Commission is self-sustaining. In 1951 an act of legislature provided that ten per cent of the gross receipts provided from television, radio, and movies, where a boxing or wrestling event is shown, should go to the Commission. This has provided the Commission with the income to build the organization which now supervises boxing and wrestling in the State of Maryland.

The entire purpose of the State Athletic Commission is to uphold high standards of sportsmanship in wrestling and boxing and to protect the public from all possibilities of illegal gambling and racketeering within these sports. To do this, all ticket handlers, announcers, and referees are under the supervision of the State Athletic Commission and their salaries are paid by the State Athletic Commission. The Commission also has an obligation to the contestants and furnishes medical supervision for both wrestling and boxing.

The Maryland State Athletic Commission also establishes standards and rules which regulate the sports and it provides an inspection system to enforce these regulations. The Commission hears all infringements of these regulations and has the power to punish infractions with suspension or fine.

RECORD OF ACCOMPLISHMENT

The Maryland State Athletic Commission has been recognized throughout the country for its achievements and many other states have patterned their athletic agency after it. The Commission was instrumental in bringing accident and life insurance to boxers and has introduced medical standards that have become a standard throughout the country.

The Commission has contributed in many ways to the public good which are not necessarily directly connected to the supervision of boxing or wrestling. In recent years the Commission worked out a plan to give wrestling shows for the inmates of the Maryland State Penitentiary. These have been tremendously successful and at the Warden's request these shows will be continued twice yearly.

Through the efforts of the State Athletic Commission, also, a good many wrestling and boxing shows have been held for charitable causes. These shows have been put on in all parts of the state and have been conducted with the same high standards as regular professional bouts.

The Maryland State Athletic Commission has also done a great deal to foster an interest in boxing and wrestling. The Commission has always maintained that an active and close relationship with the press has helped to stimulate public interest in these sports. The Commission has worked either directly or indirectly with all civic groups who have an interest in boxing or wrestling.

The Military Department

In the period from 1951 through 1958 the reorganization of the Maryland National Guard following World War II has been fully accomplished. The State of Maryland at the request of the Federal Government accepted the allocation of certain military units which, together with other units in the Commonwealth of Virginia, would constitute the 29th Division. In addition, Maryland was allocated one Transportation Battalion, two Antiaircraft Artillery Battalions and six Air units.

The 683rd and 684th Missile Battalions (NIKE) have been organized, each with a strength of approximately 400 officers and men, for the defense of the Baltimore-Washington area. These battalions are actually assigned defense missions.

STRENGTH AND ORGANIZATION

In January 1951 the strength of the Maryland National Guard, both Army and Air, had reached 4515, and 68 Army type units in addition to the Air National Guard, consisting of the 104th Fighter-Interceptor Squadron and the 104th Weather Flight, had been organized. These units were distributed throughout 34 separate cities and towns of Maryland.

The January 1, 1958 strength of the National Guard in both branches was: Army - 5928 and Air - 934, or a total of 6862 officers, warrant officers and enlisted men. This increase in personnel over the past seven years is the direct result of a concerted effort made toward better public relations, and the publication, broadcasting, and televising of material presenting the background and history of the National Guard in order to "sell" the National Guard to the people of the State.

TRAINING

Members of the Maryland National Guard continue to train under directives laid down by federal authorities. In addition to the 48 weekly drills and 15 days training in Camp annually, the officers and enlisted men may attend service schools and participate in other training programs. In a continued effort to maintain a high training standard, a total of approximately 287 officers and 311 enlisted men of the Army National Guard and 46 officers and 65 airmen of the Air National Guard have attended service schools during the past eight years. An annual average of 175 officers and 700 enlisted personnel have participated in extension school programs.

HOUSING AND CONSTRUCTION

With few exceptions the units of the Maryland National Guard are housed in state-owned armories. Since World War II all the old armories have been rehabilitated and 11 new armories have been constructed. Plans and specifications for three additional new armories have been approved by federal and state authorities, and state funds are available for their construction which is being delayed awaiting receipt of federal contributions.

In 1950 the Federal Government purchased Camp Ritchie, for which it paid $2,350,000. After a deduction of $500,000 from this amount for the purchase of a State Hospital, the remainder was made available to the Military Department and, together with other funds appropriated by the Legislature and federal contributions, was sufficient to enable us to pursue our Construction Program to the point where practically all our needs have been satisfied.

OUTSIDE USE OF ARMORIES AND FACILITIES

In 1951 the Military Department had 26 armories and 1 hangar located throughout the counties and the City of Baltimore. By 1958 this number had increased to 36 armories and 2 hangars.

While our armories are constructed primarily for the use of the National Guard units housed therein, they also play an important role in the community life of Baltimore City and the counties, as they are continuously used for social and civic affairs.

The rentals derived from the armories amount to approximately $60,000 annually. This money is reported to the Treasurer of the State and is made available for supplementing the military budget.

REVENUES AND FISCAL MATTERS

The annual State Budget for the operating expenses of the Military Department is a little in excess of $800,000, approximately $90,000 of which is derived from federal contributions and $60,000 from Armory Rentals. The State has also appropriated during the past eight years $2,549,000 for the construction and rehabilitation of armories and other military facilities throughout the State.

Supplementing these State funds, the Federal Government has contributed over the same period approximately $24,000,000 in support of the Guard Units for training, supply and construction.

For the Army Units this amounted to approximately $12,000,000 for training and supply, and approximately $4,000,000 for construction; and for the Air Components approximately $4,000,000 for training and supply, and $4,000,000 for new facilities at the Martin Airport.

PEACETIME MISSION OF THE NATIONAL GUARD

In an emergency of any kind, the primary mission of the National Guard is to defend the State against any enemy and protect vital installations throughout the state. Having accomplished its primary mission, the National Guard will assist Civil Defense in every possible manner. Only when the Governor declares martial law will the National Guard assume authority.

The Civil Defense Section of the Military Department keeps close liaison and cooperates fully with Civil Defense authorities, and in several instances has supervised those units of the Guard ordered to active duty in an emergency.

USE OF GUARD IN CIVIL EMERGENCIES

At Chestertown, on 16 July 1954, a series of explosions spread death and destruction throughout a wide area of the community. Of 300 employees of the Kent Manufacturing Plant, 11 were killed and approximately 70 injured. Company G of the 115th Infantry immediately responded and assisted in every possible manner. The armory was opened and used as both a hospital and a kitchen and material assistance was rendered.

On 18 February 1958 at Ellicott City the authorities of Howard County appealed for help because of the emergency caused by the unusually heavy snowstorm. Headquarters Company, 121st Engineer (c) Battalion responded. Approximately 40 members of this unit volunteered for service. A little later, when warranted by the hazardous conditions, heavy equipment was moved from Havre de Grace during the night by men of the 729th Ordnance Battalion.

AIR NATIONAL GUARD

On 1 January 1951, the Air National Guard of Maryland consisted of the 104th Fighter Squadron and a Limited Forecasting Flight—a total

"Smallwood's Retreat" restored home of Revolutionary General near LaPlata.

strength of approximately 450. By July 1954, the members of the 104th Fighter Squadron had achieved a high degree of proficiency by flying over 6,000 hours annually. Recruiting, pilot training, and ground crew training were stressed and successfully accomplished. During this period the unit won a gunnery trophy in competition at the First Air National Guard Gunnery meet.

The Squadron was also awarded the Spaatz Trophy for efficiency in competition with other squadrons of the Wing.

On 18 October 1953, the 8104th Replacement Training Squadron was formed with an authorized strength of 25 officers and 75 airmen.

During the period of 1953 to 1955 the 104th Fighter Squadron faced the most serious problem encountered since it was organized in 1921. Propeller-driven aircraft had become obsolete, and even though the Air Force had modern jet aircraft available for assignment to the 104th, the runways at Harbor Field were not adequate for jet operation. A split operation was conducted temporarily whereby five "Saber-jet" aircraft were maintained at Andrews Air Force Base and five maintained at Friendship International Airport, while the Squadron continued to fly the obsolete propeller-driven aircraft from Harbor Field.

AIRFIELD PROBLEM SOLVED

The effort to find a new and satisfactory airfield was finally solved in July 1955 when the Martin Company agreed to the use of the Martin Airfield by our jet aircraft and gave us a lease for a site upon which to erect a new hangar. Necessary federal funds were secured in the amount of approximately $4,000,000 with which to build new facilities and extend the runway. While construction was in progress, the split operation at Friendship was discontinued July 1957 and the 104th moved to Martin Airfield. The facilities are now completed; and the 104th is flying the modern F-86H, cannon-firing, jet aircraft and has taken its place for the defense of Baltimore and Washington.

On 10 September 1955, the 8104th Replacement Training Squadron was deactivated and the 135th Air Resupply Group was organized at Harbor Field. This unit has taken over and uses the facilities at that location. The 135th now has a strength of 60 officers and 465 airmen. The recruiting and training of this group has been most successful and the unit has been rated as the number one Air Resupply Group in the United States.

On 1 January 1957, The Headquarters, Maryland Air National Guard was organized, consisting of five officers, one warrant officer, and one airman, whose mission it is to prepare plans, policies, and programs for the Air National Guard units assigned to the State.

Since 1951 the Maryland Air National Guard has grown from one major unit of 44 officers and 401 airmen, operating from Harbor Field, to two major units and four minor units, with a total strength of 115 officers and 820 airmen, operating from two major facilities, Harbor Field and Martin Airport, and flying modern up-to-date aircraft. In addition to being ready throughout this period to accomplish their wartime mission, The Air National Guard has been called upon many times to perform mercy missions such as transporting iron lung cases, the ill and injured, and participating in search and rescue operations.

GROUND FORCES

The activities of the National Guard within the State are administered by The Adjutant General, who is also the Ranking Line Officer and controls the appropriations for the Department made by the Legislature. He is also charged with the care and control of the armories located throughout the State and the maintenance of all military records pertaining to the State Militia and with correspondence with federal authorities pertaining to the National Guard.

The Military Department includes a group of Staff Officers and enlisted men designated as the State Headquarters Detachment which has been organized on a General Staff basis in order to best employ the National Guard in any type of emergency including an atomic attack.

Comprehensive histories of the 175th Infantry Regiment, the 115th Infantry Regiment and the 110th and 224th Field Artillery Battalions, have been published.

Public Service Commission

The function of the Public Service Commission is the regulation and control of public utilities and carriers operating in Maryland and, concisely stated, it is the Commission's duty to see that the utilities and carriers render safe and adequate service at reasonable rates.

The general work of the Commission has continued with increased volume during this seven-year period. Cases entered during 1951-58 were: Formal Docket, 383; Correspondence Docket, 1,750 and Short Notice and Reparation Docket, 258, making a total of 2,391.

In addition to the cases included in the above summary, 3,917 informal complaints were received and investigated and literally thousands of oral inquiries relating to some phase of utility regulation were handled. Just as an indication of the volume of oral inquiries, the Commission, during the twelve-month period ended February 28, 1958, handled about 1,650 such inquiries relating to transportation service alone.

The law provides that no gas meter or electric meter may be put in use unless it has been inspected and sealed by the Commission, and during the seven-year period the engineers and inspectors of the Commission tested or supervised the testing of 395,085 gas meters and 534,570 electric meters.

In this time, engineering investigations, inspections and meter testing involved 1,920 trips and 2,683 days in field work, covering 263 cities and towns in Maryland and 34 towns in adjacent States. The members of the Commission's accounting staff, during this period, made 88 investigations with respect to increased rate proposals of the utilities and carriers.

In addition, the staff made 149 visits to see that utilities and carriers were following proper accounting procedures and were otherwise conforming to the requirements of law and the Commission's rules.

HIGHER RATES REQUESTED

In this seven-year period all the major utilities and carriers, as well as a very high percentage of the smaller ones, have been before the Commission in some kind of proceeding. At the present time there are 210 utilities and carriers reporting to the Commission. This does not include the 202 owners of the 1,151 taxicabs authorized to operate in Baltimore City.

Most of the utilities, including the larger ones, have sought higher rates. Many of them, during the seven-year period, have repeatedly sought increased rates to meet the ever-increasing costs of operation and to maintain earnings at a proper level. These requests were made so that they could successfully compete in the money market to obtain the huge amounts of capital to finance new construction required to provide the plant and facilities necessary to meet demands for service.

EXPANSION OF FACILITIES

A constant endeavor of the Commission is to see that utility services are made available to more and more people to meet their every need, and as the years pass, there is not only an increasing number of users but a steady increase also in the use per capita.

The output of utilities has grown almost beyond belief. In the case of one of the larger utilities, supplying both gas and electric services, electric sales increased from 2,965,307,000 kilowatt hours in 1950 to 4,882,391,-000 in 1957, an increase of about 65%, and for the same period gas sales increased from 11,105,320,000 to 31,210,456,000 cubic feet, or about 181%.

Electric customers in Maryland increased from 628,172 at the end of

1950 to 854,970 at the end of 1957, and in the same period gas customers increased from 385,499 to 524,148, about 36% for each.

Telephones in service went from 650,666 to 1,089,134, an increase of about 67%.

RATE INCREASES KEPT LOW

Since January 1, 1951, the major gas, electric and telephone utilities have proposed increases at various times estimated to produce, in the aggregate, over $30,000,000 of additional revenue a year than would be produced by the rates in effect at the time the proposals were submitted. The Commission, however, was able to hold those rate increases to about $18,000,000 on an annual basis, thereby saving for the customers for those utilities alone well over $12,000,000 a year. The cumulative effect of this saving at once can be seen. The latest utility rate case was decided by the Commission on July 14, this year. The Baltimore Gas & Electric Company requested an increase of $9,951,000 in rates charged for gas, electricity and steam. The company was allowed a rise of $9,251,000, a saving of $700,-000 to the consumer. However, at the time of this report this case is still pending review by the courts.

Transportation service and operations in the more populated areas of Maryland, including Baltimore and the surrounding territory served by lines of The Baltimore Transit Company and the areas of Montgomery and Prince George's Counties constituting the Maryland portion of Washington Metropolitan Area, have made increasing demands upon the Commission's time.

A great deal of attention has been given to these matters, and recent years have seen the Baltimore system change from one which was almost exclusively rail to what is now a motor bus and trolley bus operation, with the exception of two major lines and part of another. The Company repeatedly has been before the Commission for fare increases and service changes and, due to declining use and increasing costs, locally as well as nationwide, the problem really has been one of keeping the system in business.

JOINT COMMISSION

Conditions in the Washington Metropolitan Area also have attracted considerable attention and also have made demands on the Commission's time and efforts. The General Assembly of Maryland recognized the problem and, by Joint Resolution No. 12 of the 1954 Session, provided for the establishment of a Joint Commission to Study Passenger Carrier Facilities and Services in the Washington Metropolitan Area to consist of three members from each jurisdiction, i.e., Maryland, the District of Columbia and Virginia.

It is expected that a final report will be available this year, and it is gratifying to note that the Public Service Commission of Maryland, through participation by one of its members, has made a real contribution to what undoubtedly will be an important and lasting step in bringing about co-ordinated regulation of transit operations in the area, resulting in tremendous benefit to the residents and business concerns located in the Maryland portions of the area.

Department of Motor Vehicles

Many improvements have been made in the Department since January, 1951, to both benefit and protect the public and to expedite the routine departmental functions. Most important, many of these improvements have been installed with the end result of a large saving of the taxpayer's dollar.

In this report, only the major changes have been singled out for more detailed description. These follow:

Discontinuance of special license plates, which not only has eliminated "special privileges" and "favoritism," but has simplified the entire system and expedited service to the public. There was a complete revision of the registration system from straight numerical to a combination of letters and figures.

Consolidation of the operation at the Title Department windows, whereby an applicant now may apply at only one window, instead of three, thus reducing the waiting time to a minimum.

Furnishing of a self-addressed envelope with applications for renewal of license plates, which has proven a convenience to the public in returning applications at an early date, thus avoiding the usual last minute rush.

The appointment of a Personnel Manager and the creation of a centralized Personnel Division.

Inauguration of "in-service" training courses for all Motor Vehicle License Examiners, including recruits; and the adoption of a "point system" for the examination of applicants for driving licenses. Through legislation the valid period of Instruction and Examination Permits was extended from 30 to 60 days.

Replacement of obsolete eye-testing equipment by modern instruments.

Installation of modern filing system for traffic records.

Charles Street connecting with Harrisburg Expressway at Joppa Road.

Installation of latest devices for photostating and delivering copies of drivers' records to the Traffic Court, police authorities and other concerned agencies.

Appointment of an Assistant Registrar of Titles for better supervision and greater efficiency.

Redesign of tag applications to speed procedure.

Replacing of rented accounting machines with State-owned equipment, effecting a saving of $10,000 a year.

Microfilming of all titles in files for ten years or more, providing much needed space for other purposes.

Adoption of a standard-sized license plate—six inches by 12 inches.

With $120,000 available for the acquisition of land, and $30,000 for architects' fees, sites are being studied for a much-needed new Department building, with adequate work space and examination grounds for license applicants.

CLAIMS FUND

The Unsatisfied Claims and Judgment Fund, established by the Legislature of 1957, the Financial Responsibility Law and the re-registration of operators are administered from rented space at 33 Hopkins Place.

A separate Division was established exclusively for Title Services and Dealers, in order that they may secure registration plates as well as titles from this one Division. This system has been a benefit to the general public, as well as the Dealers and Title Services, the service to each having been expedited.

Through legislation, a Division to license all commercial Driving Training Schools has been established, which gives the Department a better control, not only over the schools and their instructors, but over the type of demonstrations given. The Department now requires the filing of Financial Responsibility Insurance by these schools, which affords the public greater protection in the event of an accident.

An Act of the 1957 Legislature provided for the gradual re-registration of all licenses to operate motor vehicles, except chauffeurs. Files will ultimately be cleared of all licensees who have moved from the State, died or no longer drive.

Commissioner of Personnel

The purposes of the Merit System Law, under which the Commissioner of Personnel operates, are "to provide candidates for appointment to positions in the classified service after determining by practical tests of the fitness of such candidates for the positions which they seek, without regard to the political or religious opinions or affiliations of such candidates, or of any other standard except the business efficiency of the classified service, and to provide adequate means for the prompt removal from positions in the classified service of all persons therein who may be indolent, incompetent, inefficient, or otherwise unfit to remain therein.

"Also to keep in a workable state the provisions for the promotion of employees as provided in this Article to the end that the same shall be so administered as to attract the best class of candidates to the classified service."

A determined effort has been made to improve the efficiency of the Department as well as to promote the efficiency of all State personnel.

A report on the activities of the Department can be only a partial report on personnel administration, since the results of its activities must be evaluated on the achievements resulting from its assistance to State departments.

From 1951 to the present time, there has been a tremendous expansion of the Mental Hygiene and State Health Department hospitals, of the roads program and of other State facilities, which has resulted in an increase in the number of new positions and employees.

When new positions are established, they must be studied and classified by this department. The number of studies of new positions increased from 382 in 1951 to 1,358 in 1957, and the number of Classified employees increased from 11,022 in 1951 to 15,622. Applications were received from 13,718 applicants in 1951 as compared to 17,506 in 1957, and the number of tests increased from 1,005 to 1,772.

TESTING PROGRAM SPEEDED

As the result of the demand for additional employees as well as for replacements, it was deemed necessary to speed up the testing program. This was attained partly by instituting an open-continuous testing program which helped to prevent the necessity for authorizing temporary appointments pending examinations and to establish eligible lists from which appointments could be made.

Major attention was paid to the recruiting of qualified applicants. This was accomplished by advertising in newspapers and professional journals, by the use of radio and television, by the distribution of posters and by urging State employees, by monthly bulletins, to secure applicants. Due to the effectiveness of the examination and recruiting programs, there are few vacancies in the State service except in difficult recruiting classes such as stenographers, nurses, doctors, etc. The number of appointments has increased from 4,662 in 1951 to 6,300 in 1957.

The Classification Division, in addition to the study of new positions, received many requests for the restudy of existing positions. Many of such requests for restudy were due to a desire for higher salaries and not to increased duties. This desire for higher salaries created what was considered a "salary problem."

State employees received general salary increases effective July 1, 1951, July 1, 1953 and October 3, 1956. For the latter increase, The General Assembly of 1956 directed that the funds provided for such adjustment be used to provide an increase from Scale 1 through Scale 28 of at least $260 for all State employees, additional increases for difficult recruiting classes, elimination of salary differential, and for a five day, forty hour, work week. After funds had been provided for the forty hour work week and an increase of $260 for each employee in Scale 1 through Scale 28, there was little money left to provide additional increases for difficult recruiting classes since it was deemed advisable to make this increase effective in October 1956.

RE-ADJUSTMENT OF SALARIES

Subsequent to the effective date of this increase, requests for adjustments in salary scales continued. These requests resulted in the Standard Salary Board adopting a Resolution on January 16, 1957 to provide that a State-wide salary study, similar to that made in 1950, be made by the Commissioner of Personnel. The purpose of such a survey was to place all job classifications in their proper salary relationship to each other.

The services of Mr. James Watson, Director of the National Civil Service League, were engaged as Consultant. Under his guidance, a comprehensive study of the salary problem was made, and the report of that study with recommendations was presented to the Standard Salary Board on October 31, 1957 for its action. After consideration, the Standard Salary Board adopted Plan 2, one of the salary plans recommended in the report, and advised the Governor of its action.

The board recommended the Governor approve Salary Plan 2 and place sufficient funds in the budget to put the plan into operation, with the understanding the Board retained the right to adjust salaries contained therein, either up or down, prior to the effective date, so long as such changes did not exceed the amount of money appropriated. The Governor approved the action of the Salary Board and included sufficient funds in the budget.

Of the $3,300,000 placed in the budget for that purpose, the General Assembly left only $500,000 for salary adjustments. The Plan, therefore, cannot become effective until May or June of 1959.

OFFICE CHANGES NAME

During the period under consideration, a study was made of the Office of the Commissioner of Personnel. In November, 1952, a report of the Governor's Commission on Administrative Organization of the State entitled "Personnel Administration in Maryland," with its findings and recommendations, was made. As a result of this report, the following changes, either by legislation or policy, were made to strengthen the Merit System:

1. A change in the name of the Department from Department of State Employment and Registration to Commissioner of Personnel.
2. Provision for filling without delay, technical, professional and administrative jobs when a qualified applicant is found by means of immediate testing.
3. Establishment of the Central Payroll Bureau with the provision that employees be paid every two weeks rather than semi-monthly or monthly.
4. Provision for a systematic manner of removal of names from eligible lists of persons who have been certified to five different vacancies and who have not been selected.
5. Improved recruiting program
6. Extension of open-continuous testing program

Since 1951, there has been additional legislation designed for the efficiency and economy of the State service, some of which follows:

1. Provision for assistance in the testing and placement of handicapped persons in the State service, and abolishment of requiring waivers to retirement membership.
2. Provision for the elimination of payment of annual and sick leave to persons employed less than six months, and for payment of terminal leave (accrued vacation) on a calendar day basis.
3. Provision for the denial of salary increments, if approved by the Commissioner, as the result of extended probation, disciplinary suspensions and recommendation of the department head.
4. Reorganization of the Standard Salary Board with the Commissioner of Personnel as Chairman of such Board.

5. Amendment of the over-time provision and vacation leave benefits on a graduated scale.
6. Provision for employees to answer unsatisfactory reports filed by department heads, and to request hearings on disciplinary suspensions aggregating fifteen days or more in a calendar year.
7. Provision for the presentation of seniority awards to employees with ten or more years of service.

WHITMORE REPORT

The Whitmore Report, by a sub-committee of the Committee on Taxation and Fiscal Matters, was made to the Legislative Council on November 14, 1956 and contained certain recommendations, among which were the recommendations for a stronger professional staff supported by clerical personnel to make a continuing study of salaries, the designation of an individual in each department to maintain liaison with the Commissioner and an effective training program to improve standards of performance within the State service.

The Commissioner of Personnel had considered the establishment of an advisory council and, prior to the Whitmore Report, had requested the personnel managers of six of the largest State departments to serve on such a council to consult with him on the varied personnel problems. The first meeting was held in December, 1956, and since that time, meetings have been held once each month or more often when necessary. Problems involving personnel administration have been discussed.

For years, the Commissioner of Personnel had recommended the employment of a Training Supervisor to work with State agencies so that adequate personnel training and counseling could be carried on, but he had been unable to obtain budgetary authority for such a position. However, funds have been made available for the initiation of a training program, and a Director of Training has been appointed.

Another major accomplishment was the revision of the Merit System Rules in June 1955. This was the first revision since 1937. Plans have been made to maintain the Rules up to date with the current Law.

The Department has three major projects:

1. Continuation of current salary information to supplement the Statewide salary study.
2. Institution of an effective training program.
3. Continuation of meetings with the Personnel Advisory Council for discussion of improvements. It is necessary to improve methods and procedures to keep up with the multitude of duties in connection with the administration of a personnel program.

The Standard Salary Board

Following a study by the Commissioner of Personnel, the Standard Salary Board adopted revised salary scales, and a new plan, containing a small general salary increase went into effect on July 1, 1951. Two scales, one for use in the institutions and another for use in the departments, were created under the new plan. The institutional scale, which was generally one scale higher than that for the same class used in departments, was based on factors of a six-day work week, remote location of institutions, and unusual and unpleasant working conditions.

A report was published by the Advisory Committee to the Commissioner on Administrative Personnel in November, 1952, entitled "Personnel Administration in Maryland." It recommended that a Division of Salary Administration be established and the Salary Board be reorganized to consist of a five-member board of public members to act only in an advisory capacity. The General Assembly of 1953 adopted part of the recommendation and amended the law by reorganizing the Board to consist of five public members appointed by the Governor with the Chief Deputy Comptroller, the Director of the Budget and the Commissioner of Personnel as ex-officio members to act in an advisory capacity without the privilege of voting.

GENERAL SALARY INCREASE GRANTED

The Standard Salary Board recommended a general State-wide salary increase for State employees which became effective on July 1, 1953.

In November, 1955, the Board adopted the policy of approving Social Security for State employees, amending the law to provide for overtime payments after a forty-hour work week, and recommending the general pay increase for State employees. A plan was adopted by the Board in January, 1956, for the elimination of the differential between departmental and institutional salary scales.

The proposed budget contained the sum of $4,600,000 to provide for a forty-hour work week and for a general pay increase. Opposition to and criticism of the Salary Board's plan for a general increase developed during the 1956 legislative session. A subcommittee of the House Ways and Means Committee was appointed to study the problem. As a result of that study, the Committee recommended an increase of at least $260 to the salary scale of each class from Scales #1 through #28, the elimination of the differential between institutional and departmental scales, a study of the difficult recruiting classes with a view to making a larger adjustment for such classes, and to provide for a forty-hour work week. In order that the sum of money contained in the budget would be sufficient to carry out these provisions, it was recommended that the general increase be made effective after October 1, 1956, and prior to January 1, 1957.

In the same Legislature, on recommendation of Governor McKeldin, funds were appropriated for participation by State employees in Federal Social Security. The program was approved by the employees in a special ballot.

ADJUSTMENT OF PAY SCALES

In view of the adjustments in scales which were made during 1956 to a number of classes in the State Roads Commission as the result of a survey which had been pending for about two years, and to classes of the Employment Security Department, resulting from a survey which had been pending for more than a year, and of the number of requests being received for adjustments in scales for classes in other departments, it was determined that the general salary increase should be made effective October 3, 1956. It also was found possible to add money, in addition to the $260 increase, to some of the most difficult recruiting classes.

The General Assembly of 1956 also reorganized the Standard Salary Board and designated the Commissioner of Personnel as Chairman of that Board. The law further provided that the Commissioner of Personnel should designated one of his employees to serve as Secretary without additional compensation.

A subcommittee, known as the Whitmore Committee, of the Committee on Taxation and Fiscal Matters was appointed to investigate the policies of and the procedures followed by the Salary Board. As a result of that investigation, the Committee made a report to the Legislative Council in November, 1956, and recommended certain changes be made in the law.

The General Assembly of 1957 passed legislation to provide that amendments in salaries, made by the Standard Salary Board and approved by the Governor, cannot take effect until the next budget period except in emergency situations which are approved by the Board of Public Works.

SALARY INCREASE STUDY

Following the October 3, 1956, general salary increase, the Standard Salary Board was deluged with requests for adjustments in salary scales, and the Board, on January 16, 1957, adopted a Resolution directing the Commissioner of Personnel to make a study, similar to that made in 1950, in order that inequities in salaries might be corrected, and freezing salaries for the period of such study. The salary study was made, and the report with two suggested salary plans was presented to the Salary Board in October, 1957. The Salary Board adopted Plan #2 and recommended to the Governor that he place a sufficient amount of money in the budget to make it effective on July 1, 1958. The Board reserved the right, however, to make any change in the scales, either upwards or downwards, prior to the effective date. The recommendation of the Board was adopted by the Governor, and the money was placed in the budget for consideration by the 1958 General Assembly. However, the General Assembly left only $500,000 in the budget for this purpose. It, therefore, will not be possible to place the plan in operation until late in the 1959 fiscal year.

State Tax Commission

The growth of the State Tax Commission might best be illustrated by the increase in the assessable basis for computing taxes for the years 1950 through 1958 and the increase in the number of foreign and domestic corporations for the same period, as revealed by the following tabulation:

Year	*Assessable Basis for State Purposes*	*Total Corps. For. and Dom.*
1950	$4,560,079,076	18,908
1951	4,985,955,790	19,673
1952	5,534,882,786	21,011
1953	5,769,236,010	22,639
1954	6,189,986,759	24,756
1955	6,489,209,332	26,779
1956	7,206,940,899	28,535
1957	7,853,585,000	30,256
1958	8,141,313,000 est.	not final

The increasing activity of the State Tax Commission from 1951 to date is indicated by the amount of money collected by the Commission from domestic and foreign corporations for bonus tax, recording fees, dissolution fees, qualifying fees, etc. In 1951 the total amount collected from domestic corporations was $424,661.03; in 1957, the total amount collected from domestic corporations was $615,995.47. In 1951 the total amount collected from foreign corporations was $65,293.50, and in 1957, $91,361.50.

UNIFORMITY OF ASSESSMENTS

While the assessing of property is not an exact science, it must ever be the objective of assessors and those supervising the assessors to strive for fair, accurate and uniform assessments. The State Tax Commission feels that there has been a great improvement in the assessing of property in Maryland during the years 1951 through 1957, and that assessments are now much more uniform than they were in 1951.

In 1953 a committee of some of the most experienced of the Maryland assessors conducted a survey to determine the level of assessments in the 23 Counties and Baltimore City. After a comprehensive study, the committee reported that in one County the ratio of assessments to sales was as low as 25%, and in Baltimore City the ratio of assessments to sales was 60%; the other Counties ranged between those two figures.

The ratio of assessments to sales on a State-wide basis was 40%. At present, the lowest County has a ratio of 38%, and the State-wide average is 49.7%.

Despite the gains revealed by the aforegoing data, the State Tax Commission, collaborating with its supervisors of assessments in the various Counties, has plans for further improvement, some of which have already been translated into action.

TAX MAP DEPARTMENT

In 1951 the General Assembly passed a law authorizing the preparation and installation for each County of a "record of properties and system of appraisal aids, consisting of property location maps and unit land values."

Pursuant to this law, the State Tax Commission set up a Tax Map Department. There are now 27 employees in this department, 24 of whom are draftsmen.

Immediately upon receiving the above mentioned statutory authorization from the General Assembly, the task was started of compiling approximately 1,600 maps covering the State of Maryland, showing roads, rivers, etc. In accordance with an agreement with the United States Department of Agriculture, aerial photographs were taken of the entire State. Simultaneously, arrangements were made with the officials of the various Counties to accumulate an index of the deeds for each individual property owner.

These deeds were microfilmed, so that property line description could be plotted on the maps to show each individual parcel of ownership. This plotting is being done on approximately 700,000 pieces of property in the State, and almost 3,000,000 deeds are being plotted. Ink tracings of these maps have been made, so that they can be reproduced for the use of county assessors and other State and County agencies, particularly the State Roads Commission and County Planning and Zoning Boards.

To date, more than 85% of the area of the State has been covered by these tax maps; the area still to be covered lies chiefly in Baltimore, Anne Arundel and Prince George's Counties.

These tax maps will be of great assistance in improving the quality of assessments, making for greater accuracy and uniformity. These tax maps will give the county assessor a more comprehensive picture of his area than he has ever had before.

He will be able to weigh the various aspects of the value of the land in his County, such as its use, shape and positive location, its relation to the surrounding community and the effect of surrounding economic changes upon the land. Maryland may take pride in the fact that it was the first State to plan a comprehensive mapping program.

State Insurance Department

From the period 1951 through 1958, many major accomplishments have been achieved in the Maryland State Insurance Department. Great strides have been made in the regulatory control of the insurance business and increased protection for the public.

In addition to the normal growth of the life insurance companies in the State, many of them have entered the accident and health insurance field during the last several years. To properly review all policies submitted by these companies, the actuarial staff has been enlarged by the addition of two actuaries. Because of the rapid growth of these accident and health companies, it has been necessary to request the enactment of many regulatory bills. Many of these bills are now laws and form an important part of the Maryland Insurance Code.

Among other regulatory matters approved was the entering of Maryland Hospital Service, Inc., and Maryland Medical Service, Inc., (Blue Cross and Blue Shield) into the "non-group" field in Maryland, thus providing coverage for individuals heretofore not eligible.

Many important rate adjustments have been made regarding fire and casualty insurance during the period. In August of 1953 a new form of Multiple Line Package Policy for an indivisible premium was approved, designated "Homeowners" policies, Forms A and B. These policies provide insurance in package form for fire, extended coverage, additional living expense, residence burglary and comprehensive personal liability, all for an indivisible premium determined basically by the amount of fire insurance to be carried on the dwelling.

August 15, 1957, marked the inception of a new form of insurance coverage in Maryland—the Industrial Property Policy Program, which was approved by the Insurance Commissioner. Subject to specified exclusions and limitations, it makes available to industrial enterprises, insurance against all risks of direct physical loss of or to stocks of goods, wares and merchandise in a single insurance policy.

Among the important rulings issued by the Insurance Commissioner in recent years were the following of lasting importance to the State:

A ruling issued in accordance with the recommendation of the National Association of Insurance Commissioners to all licensed companies in the State writing Accident and Health Insurance, regarding the advertising of accident or sickness coverages. This has been most beneficial to Maryland policyholders because it has eliminated the dissemination of misleading descriptions of benefits in advertisements and descriptive circulars of insurance policies.

A ruling requiring all companies writing finance accounts to furnish detailed information for the purpose of correcting a situation which indicated that there had been abuses in the classification of collision insurance written in connection with the financing of private passenger automobiles. This office received more than 600 complaints from Maryland policyholders regarding alleged misclassifications. All policies submitted were checked, and through the cooperation of the individual insurers, it was possible to adjust all misclassified policies.

In February, 1957, all companies writing automobile liability insurance were informed that the practice of demanding requests for insurance cancellations, merely because the insurer wished to escape the risk, would not be tolerated. This practice, in which some insurers had engaged, penalized the insured by cancelling his policy on a short rate, rather than in a pro-rata basis.

FIRE MARSHAL'S OFFICE

The Fire Marshal's Office of the State Insurance Department expanded during this period and there are now five full-time fire investigators, in addition to approximately 50 Special Deputy Fire Marshals who serve throughout the State on a voluntary basis. This expansion has facilitated the regular inspection of hospitals, nursing homes, child care homes, institutions and places of public gathering in the State in order to ascertain that all reasonable fire safety precautions are being complied with, and this has reduced greatly fire hazards throughout the State.

Rulings have been issued by the Commissioner amending and strengthening existing Explosives Regulations, and very strict control has been exercised over fireworks displays in the State. Through such control in Maryland, there has been a major reduction in the injuries—fatal and non-fatal—to the citizens.

A major accomplishment was the complete reorganization in the Licensing Bureau of the Insurance Department. It enables the issuance of more than 40,000 renewal insurance licenses from the period April 1 to June 30 each year. The reorganization has facilitated uniformity in records and licenses, as well as more rapid processing of applications as they are received.

An examination was made of the laws of the 47 states and the District of Columbia with regard to premium taxes and license fees charged by the various states. This has made effective the retaliatory provisions of the Maryland Law with respect to these fees and has resulted in increased revenue to the State. Premium tax forms have been revised by this office, and this revision should result in more accuracy.

In 1951 receipts for the Maryland Insurance Department were approximately four and one-half million dollars. It is estimated that in 1958 our collections will exceed eight million dollars.

The Department continues its careful and detailed examination of companies licensed to do business in Maryland in order to ascertain their solvency and that they continue to fulfill their obligations to policyholders.

Bank Commissioner

During the period from January 1st, 1951 through December 31st, 1957, the following material changes have occurred in the various classes of the financial institutions under the Department's control which is indicative of the growth of our State financially during this era:

	1951	*1957*
Number of Banking Institutions	103	98
Number of Branches	114	166
Number of Credit Unions	41	47
Number of Industrial Finance Licensees	111	190
Total Resources of the Banking Institutions	1,467,069,504.00	1,931,713,070.47
Total Resources of the Credit Unions	4,512,310.60	16,660,269.32
Total Resources of the Industrial Finance Licensees	48,316,326.36	94,140,998.43*

* As of 12-31-56

From these figures it will be observed that the resources of the Banking Institutions from January 1st, 1951 to December 31, 1957 showed a total growth of $464,643,566.47 or 31 per cent; Credit Unions $12,147,958.72 or 269 per cent; Industrial Finance Licensees $45,824,-672.07 or 93 per cent.

DEPARTMENT BECOMES SELF-SUSTAINING

The Fiscal Year ending June 30th, 1957, was the first in which the revenue from the Departmental activities exceeded the general appropriation in the Budget, thus placing the Department on a self-sustaining basis.

During this 7-year period under general routine the Department considered and approved 68 charter amendments to the various charters of the existing Banking Institutions and at the same time there were 12 mergers which came before the Department for study, consideration and final approval. During this period the Department conducted 2,327 regular examinations of the financial institutions under its supervision, aside from hundreds of special visits following specific complaints.

In 1951, on the recommendation of the Bank Commissioner, the General Assembly passed a Bank Merger Act. During this same year the Assembly also passed, on the recommendation of the Bank Commissioner, a Dormant Account Statute and in 1955, the Assembly amended the Statutes of Maryland dealing with branches of Mutual Savings Institutions upon the recommendation of the Bank Commissioner to permit State-wide branch banking of such institutions.

State Auditor

This department makes post-audits of the various financial operations of the State agencies, departments and collectors of revenue resulting in the determination and assessment of additional revenue, the detection and assistance with the examination of deficiencies, shortages or the unauthorized withholding of State funds, resulting in the recovery of funds from the persons or agencies involved, or from insurance companies, thus accomplishing the result of safeguarding, determining and recovering additional State revenue and funds.

A number of recommendations have been made by this office during the past eight years which culminated in legislation that has resulted in and will continue to effect considerable savings of money to the State.

Some of the tangible results with regard to recoveries determined by the audit work of this office, upon which this office has engaged in or was consulted with, amounted to approximately $207,000, involving 39 departments, agencies or other governmental units of the State.

However, the successful operation of this office is not measured entirely by the amounts of money recovered from shortages, etc., but the prime objectives of the office are the prevention of losses to the State, the determination of proper agency operations within the limits of their budgets, etc., the verification that collections are effected properly and accounted for, and that the distributions of these collections are made in accordance with the provisions of the Public General Laws of Maryland and that the reports of our findings in connection with these functions are made to the proper legal authorities.

IMPROVED ACCOUNTING SYSTEMS

The office also has assisted in making improvements in the accounting systems of the State agencies and departments, as well as conferring with department heads, in connection with the installation of modern accounting machines for the purpose of improving the expedition of the accounting, internal auditing controls and reporting work of the State's fiscal activities.

This office also, in accordance with the law and with the approval of the Board of Public Works, has made two examinations of the overseas operations of the College of Special and Continuation Studies of the University of Maryland at its headquarters at Heidelberg, Germany.

The auditing personnel of the office, with the exception of the State Auditor and the Deputy State Auditor, was placed under the Merit System as of June 1, 1951. This provision is attracting capable career accountants and should assist in increasing the permanence of qualified auditors.

The department has been successful and is continuing to upgrade the experience and qualifications of the staff through the addition of certified public accountants and other trained accountants, in order to further facilitate the efficient conduct of the important and technical work of this office.

The Land Office

While this is one of the smaller agencies of the State, it is one of the most important. All land now included in the present limits of Maryland was granted to Cecil, Lord Baltimore in 1632. While this office has been a part of Maryland government, since the earliest time, the Land Office as presently constituted was established by the Constitution of 1851.

The Land Office keeps records pertaining to the boundaries of land. All warrants, certificates and patents for land since 1634 are on file with the agency. The Commissioner hears and determines all disputes which may arise concerning the validity of surveys originating in the office.

It is interesting to note that during the last seven years only two caveat proceedings were brought before the Commissioner, indicating a careful screening of all applications for the various warrants of survey. During this period, the Land Office has issued 59 patents having a composition value of $13,175.85.

At the request of the Governor, in the interests of conserving the comparatively small areas of vacant land remaining in the State, the Commissioner has adopted a policy of clearing with the Department of Forests and Parks and the Game and Inland Fish Commission lands which might have a possibility of use for wild life conservation or recreational purposes.

ADMINISTERS RECORDS

In addition to the functions outlined above, the office maintains and administers the records of the Chancery Court, plats and abstracts of deeds, mortgages and releases. Since 1951, microfilmed copies of deeds, mortgages and releases have replaced the abstracts previously submitted by the Clerks of Courts. This method has proved to be economical, practical and accurate.

The office has kept abreast of the latest technological advances in the preservation and repair of its records, laminating during the past seven years more than 28,000 pages. Providing courteous service to title and genealogical researchers has been a tradition of the Land Office.

In keeping with this long established tradition, assistance has been rendered to 2900 persons who have visited the office and approximately the same number who have written for information since 1951.

Committee to Promote Employment of the Physically Handicapped

The objectives of the Committee, which functions primarily as an educational and public relations instrument, are to create a public awareness of the problems faced by handicapped individuals in finding employment; to provide a continuing public information and education program; to cooperate with all groups, public and private, in promoting services for the handicapped; and to initiate and actively promote programs to stimulate hiring the handicapped.

In association with this sustained effort, from 1951 through 1957, the Vocational Rehabilitation Division of the Maryland Department of Education has provided effective vocational rehabilitation to 7,400 handicapped persons in the State. The Employment Service Division of the Maryland Department of Employment Security has placed successfully 12,688 handicapped persons in gainful employment. These workers thereby have been enabled to make a direct contribution to society, instead of constituting a drain upon its resources. There are indications that many others with lesser handicaps, who have no specific need for governmental services, have been impelled by this example to take heart and find places of their own in the constructive life of the community.

The Governor of Maryland is the official head of this Committee. Its membership is composed of leaders from industry, labor, education, medicine, the clergy and the state and national governments. All members serve without compensation.

The President's Committee on Employment of the Physically Handicapped acts in an advisory capacity to the Governor's Committee, as it does to states committees throughout the United States.

The accomplishments of the Maryland Committee during the past eight years have been achieved largely through such promotional and organizational vehicles as those listed below.

THE INCREASED ACTIVITY OF LOCAL COMMITTEES

So that the program for the handicapped might reach all Maryland citizens, the Governor's Committee has established a local committee in each of the State's 23 Counties and in Baltimore City. These local groups, under careful guidance, have become well organized units which initiate many of their own programs and show considerable skill in obtaining publicity for their activities.

The interest of the local committees has increased materially over the years, as is evidenced by the fact that regional meetings, sparsely attended when held originally on an annual basis, have been stepped up, at popular demand, to a semi-annual basis and now are well attended.

LOCAL PARTICIPATION IN ESSAY AND POSTER CONTESTS

The Governor's Committee sponsors a poster contest and an essay contest annually for high school juniors and seniors in all the public, private and parochial schools of Maryland. Through the work of the local committees, the faculty of every high school in the State is informed of these contests, and in 1958 the number of entries and the number of participating schools set new records for both contests. It has been the experience of the Committee that this participation provides the young citizens of our State with a meaningful awareness of the problems of handicapped persons and of the services available to them.

The winning Maryland essay is entered in the National Essay Contest each year. And while there is no national poster contest, Maryland's winning 1956 poster received national recognition after the Governor's Committee conceived the idea of displaying it as a billboard poster. The President's Committee followed suit and had thousands of copies made and distributed to committees in every state. Thus, during National Employ the Physically Handicapped Week, 1957, Maryland's contribution became a familiar billboard along the highways around the nation.

REGIONAL MEETING OF THE PRESIDENT'S COMMITTEE

On February 27, 1957, the Governor's Committee was host to a Regional Meeting of the President's Committee for representatives from New York, Pennsylvania, New Jersey, Delaware, Maryland, District of Columbia, Virginia, West Virginia, North Carolina, Puerto Rico and the Virgin Islands.

Stimulating talks were made by Governor McKeldin of Maryland, Mayor D'Alesandro of Baltimore, Committee executives and representatives of business, labor and the professions. The meeting was one of the more successful in a series conducted in various cities during the preceding two years.

"Performance," the official publication of the President's Committee, devoted the cover and five of the 14 pages of its April, 1957, issue to the Baltimore meeting.

AWARDS CONTEST

Since 1952, the Governor's Committee has sponsored an annual Awards Luncheon, at which time handicapped individuals who have made an outstanding "comeback" and Maryland employers who have utilized handicapped workers are honored by the community. Nominations for these awards are open to all local committees. Also, a Maryland physician selected by the Medical and Chirurgical Faculty of Maryland for exceptional work with the handicapped is presented a citation by the Governor and by the President's Committee. This awards program affords much publicity to both local and state committees and to the problems and successes of the handicapped generally.

State Tobacco Authority

The State Tobacco Authority regulates tobacco marketing practices and the seeking of new markets and uses for leaf tobacco produced in Maryland. These powers are granted in line with legislative policy of relieving "disturbed and confused conditions surrounding the marketing of leaf tobacco in this State."

MARKET REGULATION

Many of the practices on the markets for Maryland tobacco were found to be detrimental. This included the packing of tobacco, the display on warehouse floors, speculation on markets, changing of prices after the tobacco had been sold on the warehouse floor, changing of the designation of buyers and the operation of many irresponsible buyers on the markets.

After a careful study of market conditions and regulations in the markets for other tobacco types, the Authority, in accordance with law, has for several years promulgated regulations regarding the operation of tobacco markets in the State. In addition, the Executive Secretary and two assistants hired for the market season have given markets close supervision to make the market regulations as fully effective as possible.

While a certain amount of speculative buying is highly important to the orderly marketing of tobacco, much of the speculation which was characteristic of Maryland tobacco marketing at the beginning of this period was very detrimental to the interests of the tobacco grower. As a result of the close supervision provided by the Authority, the number of independent speculative buyers was reduced from 108 in 1954 to 37 in 1957.

MARKET PROMOTION

Maryland tobacco, being mild and low in nicotine and tars, has suffered from the tremendous growth of filter-tip cigarettes which require heavier tobaccos. This has contributed to the accumulation of excess supplies, particularly in the grade ranges that customarily are used in domestic cigarettes.

The highest smoking grades of Maryland tobacco are purchased and used principally by Swiss cigarette manufacturers. Some of these cigarettes, however, have gained substantial favor in Austria. Other grades are exported in varying and lesser quantities to several other countries.

In view of these conditions, the Authority's market promotional activities have fallen in three categories: (1) promotion of the use of Maryland tobacco by domestic cigarette companies, (2) protection and increase of outlets in Switzerland and Austria, and (3) development of new foreign outlets, particularly for tobacco in surplus supply.

Annual calls have been made on officials of the major domestic cigarette manufacturers by members of the Authority or by others for the account of this agency.

During 1951 and 1952, the Authority engaged a special "Tobacco Ambassador" to call on many tobacco manufacturers in Europe. In all, calls were made on 73 manufacturers and the good qualities of Maryland tobacco were discussed with them. These calls, without a doubt, were an important factor in the growth of Maryland tobacco purchases by these countries during this period.

FOREIGN MARKETS

The Authority has also engaged the cooperative action of the Foreign Agricultural Service of U. S. Department of Agriculture in the development of expanded foreign outlets for Maryland tobacco. This development alone seems to afford a more or less permanent outlet for more than a million pounds of Maryland tobacco per year.

Currently, the greatest need for market outlets for Maryland tobacco is in the medium and lower cigarette grades. Much more needs to be known about the contributions of these grades to the smoking qualities of cigarettes manufactured from both tropical tobaccos and other U. S. cigarette types. The University of Maryland currently has under way a panel-tester type of research project on these two subjects. The results of this research undoubtedly will provide a much broader base for market promotion with both domestic and foreign cigarette manufacturers, considering the low nicotine and tar content of Maryland tobacco.

Real Estate Commission

In early 1955 the Maryland Legislature amended the Real Estate Law in a manner which strengthened its application and also increased the scope of supervision of the Real Estate Commission. The Legislature by enacting Section 221 (d) now permits the Commission to employ two or more field inspectors, and to have the services of an attorney-at-law to conduct hearings thereby eliminating the unsatisfactory procedure of having commissioners cross-question witnesses. The field inspectors, provided with state automobiles, gather full information regarding complaints and otherwise act as goodwill link between the Commission and the licensees.

One requirement for licensing real estate brokers, which had been a loop-hole for many applicants with scanty qualifications to apply, was adequately strengthened by requiring applicants to have served two years as a licensed real estate salesman. This prerequisite has contributed in no small measure to the licensing of men better qualified to serve the public interest.

REGULATION CHANGES

Several other changes now require that copies of all documents be promptly furnished to all signers; that a broker's name, as broker or agent, appear in all of his advertisements, even though a salesman's name may appear also; that he shall not accept listings at a "net" price; and a few additional amendments of lesser moment.

Costs of the added personnel and the quarterly publishing of roster data in place of annual only were met by increasing the licensing fees. Since the number of licensees has not climbed beyond 10,000, the amount of fee increases has proven adequate to the point where $20,000 more per year goes into the General Fund than before the amendments were enacted.

The Real Estate Commission is running smoothly; it is staffed by seasoned, competent people, and the operation and results of the Commission itself proves that a 3-member commission, as is the case in nearly 70% of the states, is adequate for successful administration of the licensing act.

State Library

Since 1951 the State Library has added 7,173 bound volumes, and received approximately 70,000 pamphlets, leaflets, supplements, catalogs, and upkeep services, mostly of a temporary nature.

It has kept up to date its series of the National Reporter System; the laws, codes and reports of other states; added to the growing number the best of legal textbooks published; and started a special collection of outstanding legal philosophies, histories, essays, and other publications of interest to attorneys. The Library has increased its subscriptions to the leading legal periodicals, so that now it is receiving 110—25 percent more than received in 1951. There have been added many histories, biographies, and other books of general interest to the Reference section.

A catalog of law books in the State Library, which included a brief history of the Library, was compiled and published in 1954 and a supplement issued in 1956. This catalog has now been completely revised, and the manuscript is in the hands of the printer.

During this period the Law Library was inventoried, the card catalogs in both the Law Library and the Reference Library were thoroughly checked and revised, 600 periodicals were bound, 3,000 books rebound and 60,000 books cleaned, oiled, repaired, and mended, and approximately 50,000 volumes were moved and relocated. New cabinets for the legal periodicals and pamphlets were purchased.

FACILITIES EXPANDED

Three large display cases were specially designed and constructed and permitted the Library, for the first time, to display some of our rare books and a volume of the Audubon collection. Three handsome Bibles —Protestant, Catholic and Hebrew versions—and a lectern on which to display them, were presented to the Library, together with the Maryland and United States flags, in a ceremony attended by many State and Federal officials and dignitaries.

Two other accessions to the Library are of especial note, i. e., the files of the Baltimore Sunpapers, 1837-1941, presented by the Enoch Pratt Library, and the original census records of Maryland for 1880 presented by The National Archives and Records Service.

A great improvement in the appearance of the Library was the installation of a new vinyl plastic tile floor covering. New electric light fixtures were installed in the storage areas, the entire library was re-wired and many old electric outlets were replaced.

Aviation Commission

Since 1955, the Maryland State Aviation Commission has succeeded in securing passage of legislation placing the Commission on a self-supporting basis of operation (with a State budget of $21,500 for the fiscal year, 1959), and has charted a course—and drafted preliminary legislation—designed to give Maryland a realistic, long-range airport development program.

The Commission has analyzed the factors which have played an important role in the development of aviation throughout the United States. The eventual existence of at least one suitable publicly-owned airport (under private management) in each of the State's 23 counties is deemed mandatory. Suitable airport facilities already exist in Somerset, Wicomico, Talbot, Frederick, Washington and Allegany counties as well as at Baltimore City. The lack of proper facilities in the remaining 17 counties is considered a serious handicap to future development of aviation and business enterprises in those areas.

To take advantage of the approximately $400,000 in Federal funds earmarked annually for Maryland airport development, the Commission has drafted legislation—unsuccessfully introduced in 1958, but to be introduced again in 1959—seeking establishment of a State Airport Development Fund able to provide a portion of locally-required matching funds.

The legislation calls for an initial recoverable appropriation of $200,000 which will enable the Commission's airport development program to get under way with funds provided as follows: Federal Aid Airport Program, 50%; State Capital Improvement Program, 25%; County or Municipality participation, 25%.

GENERAL FUNCTIONS

Created in 1929, the State Aviation Commission is composed of five members appointed by the Governor for 3-year terms. The Commission assists and encourages general aviation, which is defined in terms of private flying, flight training, light aircraft charter service, business and corporate aircraft operations, agricultural aviation, aircraft maintenance and supply.

The Commission provides direct consulting service on maintenance, engineering and sound economical operation at publicly-owned, or privately-owned airports.

It registers and licenses all airports, air navigators, aeronautical schools and flight instructors, and promotes safety regulations and the construction and installation of air markers and navigational aids. The Commission also administers all federal funds provided for airport development within the State.

AIRPORT DEVELOPMENT PROGRAM

1. A deadline of June 30, 1958 existed, but has been extended, in providing necessary duplicating matching funds for $375,000 in Federal funds which have been approved for airport construction at Ocean City and in Montgomery County. Due to the failure of legislative action on the Commission's proposal for a State Airport Development Fund, the entire matching funds for these projects must now come from the counties or municipalities involved if the Federal grants are to be obtained. The status of these two programs is as follows:

Airport Site	*Matching Funds Needed*	*Progress to Date*
Ocean City	$100,000	City has option on 115-acre site, Master plan has been approved by the Commission and the Civil Aeronautics Administration.
Montgomery County	$275,000	Site selection not yet made. County hopes to raise matching funds in near future.

2. Federal funds totaling $187,000 have been matched by the city of Hagerstown for expansion of its municipal airport. The Commission has programmed $300,000 for further expansion with funds to be provided jointly by the city and Federal Government.

3. The Commission has placed applications on file for Federal funds totaling $2,497,000 for expansion and reconstruction of the Cambridge municipal airport, and for development of publicly-owned airports in Baltimore County, Prince Georges County, and Garrett County. Preliminary studies have been made for site selections in Baltimore County and Prince Georges County.

4. Initial aerial surveys have been made looking to development of publicly-owned airports in the Annapolis area, and in St. Mary's County, Calvert County, and Harford County.

5. The Commission is attempting to have the Department of Agriculture's airport at Beltsville turned over to the State.

ACTIVITIES OTHER THAN AIRPORT DEVELOPMENT

The Commission has assisted in expansion of existing commercial airports in the State from a total of 26 in 1955 to the present total of 34. An airplane flying over Maryland is now at all times within at least 40 miles of a commercial airport.

Plans have been made to install new air markers throughout the State. Funds which may be obtained over and above the Commission's operating budget will be devoted primarily for this purpose.

Arrangements made with four or five out of state concerns able to provide the latest aircraft equipment for use in agricultural seeding, fertilization, pest control, soil surveys, and erosion control.

Helped establish a Teacher's Workshop at the USAF 2611th Air Reserve Center in cooperation with Baltimore City Department of Education and the Maryland Wing, Civil Air Patrol.

Sponsored a flight safety course (the "180-degree course") for pilots which was developed at the University of Illinois Institute of Aviation.

Inaugurated an annual Maryland Aviation Conference for pilots and aircraft owners at Friendship Airport. Program includes panel discussions on aviation education, private flying, business flying, airport development, and navigational and safety aids. Attendance in 1956 was 126 persons; in 1957, 148 persons.

COMMISSION ACTIVITIES

Administered federal airport construction and expansion funds for the Hagerstown and Easton municipal airports. Completed State's financial assistance program for airport construction and expansion at Frederick, Salisbury and Crisfield.

Successfully intervened with major scheduled airlines before federal agencies to retain and expand scheduled airline service at Easton and Cumberland municipal airports.

Successfully joined with the City of Baltimore in intervention before federal agencies to have Baltimore designated as a major east-coast terminal for scheduled airline trans-Atlantic air cargo service.

Developed a plan for availability and use of privately-owned Maryland aircraft in emergency civil defense work.

Worked with federal agencies to install, or retain, radio ranges, weather service, and landing and approach aids at Harbor Field, Dundalk and the Frederick, Easton, Salisbury and Cumberland municipal airports.

Prepared and published an airport directory, special bulletins, and the newsletter, "Maryland Aero News."

Board of Motion Picture Censors

A review of the accomplishments of this Department is mainly concerned with its activities in administering the State law of Motion Picture Censorship, and the gradual development of the jurisprudence applicable thereto.

Our system of censorship, or "prior restraint," requires review and approval of motion pictures, before they can be disseminated to the public.

Prior to 1955 the decisions of the various State Boards in licensing moral and proper films, and in disapproving films which were considered sacrilegious, obscene, indecent, inhuman or immoral, or such as tended in the judgment of the Board to debase or corrupt morals or incite to crime, were based on broad considerations with varying degrees of the undefined words used in State laws. Such decisions were in part colored by the sensibilities of the locality involved and the personality of the censor. After the Burstyn decision, the Maryland Legislature realized that undefined categories were too broad and indefinite to withstand constitutional attack, and amended the law by defining the standards as follows:

1: A motion picture film or view shall be considered to be obscene if, when considered as a whole, its calculated purpose or dominant effect is substantially to arouse sexual desires, and if the probability of this effect is so great as to outweigh whatever other merits the film may possess.

2: A motion picture film or view shall be considered to be of such a character that its exhibition would tend to debase or corrupt morals if its dominant purpose or effect is erotic or pornographic; or if it portrays acts of sexual immorality, lust or lewdness, or if it expressly or impliedly presents such acts as desirable, acceptable or proper patterns of behavior.

3: A motion picture film or view shall be considered of such a character that its exhibition would tend to incite to crime if the theme or the manner of its presentation presents the commission of criminal acts or contempt for law as constituting profitable, desirable, acceptable, respectable or commonly accepted behavior, or if it advocates or teaches the use of, or the methods of use of, narcotics or habit-forming drugs.

Since then, a series of court decisions in Maryland, New York and the Supreme Court of the United States, have further evaluated "prior restraint" censorship with relation to the free speech guarantees of the Constitution, and in each instance stood ready to strike down any censorship attempt which appeared to range beyond the censors constitutional or statutory powers. These decisions confine the use of "prior restraint" within a narrower range than ever before, and thus far have held that the motion pictures involved were not of the "magnitude" contemplated by prior restraint, and were not too "rugged" for general consumption.

COURT RULINGS

The Maryland Court of Appeals applied its concept of obscenity to the motion picture "Naked Amazon" on March 7, 1957, after the Board had ordered deletions of nudity shown below the waist. The Court ruled that none of the scenes portrayed any action which was suggestive of sexual activity. Nudity they said, "is not necessarily obscene or lewd." Prior to this decision, it had been generally understood by writers and others interested in the field of Motion Picture Censorship that the impact of motion pictures on the public, was greater than other media of expression. It is noteworthy that our Court of Appeals quoted magazine and book cases, and thus placed motion pictures in the same category as the still photograph or the printed word.

Thus far, Courts have held that standards set forth in the law must be definite, but with a limited permissible discretion. The personal opinion of the censor cannot stand as a basis for "prior restraint" nor can he be arbitrary or capricious.

Several Court opinions have brought into focus the disparity between the motion picture law and the present Maryland law prohibiting youngsters from buying certain magazines. On August 12, 1957 the Board of Motion Picture Censors recommended that it be given authority to license certain films as restricted for those under 16 years of age, when such films could not otherwise be denied a license. The Attorney General of Maryland thereupon ruled that such a law would be constitutional. In furtherance of the Board's request, a bill was introduced in the 1958 session of the Legislature, but was defeated. The bill will again be presented to the Legislature in 1959.

Public Buildings and Grounds

During the past eight years this department has launched a number of new construction and rehabilitation projects in connection with the many buildings and areas under its supervision in the State Capital.

The most important improvements are listed below in concise detail:

Installation and operation of the floodlighting system of the State House dome—the subject of much favorable comment.

Complete re-slating of the roof of the new and old sections of the State House, except for the dome sections.

Replacement of the hidden gutters of the Governor's Mansion by gutters of new design preventing further seepage of water and damage to interior walls.

Construction of a parking lot, with capacity of approximately 70 automobiles, adjacent to the College Avenue Office Building.

Replacement of the antiquated coal burning installation in the State Power Plant with a complete new and modern oil burning plant and renovation of the building inside and out.

Construction of a colonial type wall and walks in and encircling the State House grounds.

Installation of a new lighting system on the State House grounds with 32 colonial Williamsburg-type lamp posts—18 being around the periphery of the Circle, and 14 at other appropriate points through the grounds, adding further to the colonial motif of the area.

Construction of a 231-car State parking lot along Bladen Street adjacent to the Power Plant, intended primarily for use of the General Assembly during its sessions, but available at other times to employees in all the State buildings.

Modification of the heating system in the State House and Court of Appeals building from steam-hot air to hot water radiators and hot water-air convectors.

Construction of an additional large State Office Building with parking lot and grounds covering the entire block bounded by Bladen, Calvert, Northwest and Carroll Streets.

Air conditioning of the Court of Appeals Building.

Aside from the above individual items, this Department performs the constant task of the maintenance, operation, cleaning, heating and cooling of the eight State buildings in Annapolis and the extensive grounds, sidewalks and parking areas connected therewith.

Psychiatric building for teen-age patients at Rosewood.

Civil Defense Agency

Technical and scientific developments in warfare, particularly atomic and hydrogen bombs and methods of delivery, have led to an ever increasing necessity that our citizens be prepared on the home-front against the possibility of war.

The Maryland Civil Defense Act of 1949 placed responsibility for Civil Defense on the Governor.

A staff of fourteen persons serve under the Director to guide and assist the political subdivisions in developing their plans and to coordinate Maryland's efforts with its neighboring States and the Federal Government. In addition the heads and various employees of many other State agencies periodically engage in Civil Defense planning, organizing and training activities under the guidance of the Maryland Civil Defense Agency.

In the event of an enemy attack these State agencies would be responsible for the major State-wide activities.

The Agency, with headquarters at the Pikesville Armory, has during the past eight years served to keep Marylanders alert to the dangers of enemy attack and at the same time developed and implemented a State Plan for Civil Defense.

At the 1951 Session of the General Assembly Governor McKeldin succeeded in securing passage of a Civil Defense bond issue for $1,000,000. Those funds and subsequent appropriations from general funds have served to provide a sizable investment in Civil Defense equipment, goods, training and public knowledge.

MEDICAL SUPPLIES STOCKPILED

A fine example of preparedness in this field is borne out by medical supplies. Stockpiled are the essentials for twenty 200-bed Emergency Hospitals owned by the State. These units can be readily moved and assembled to take care of injured in the event of attack. In addition 200 Casualty Clearing Stations are located in strategic locations throughout the State.

Civil Defense material can only be used if Marylanders, including many volunteers, are adequately trained to use them. Continuous instructional programs have been carried out by the Agency's Training Officer in cooperation with local Civil Defense organizations and other agencies, both governmental and private, such as the Red Cross. Thousands of our citizens have been trained in Civil Defense Administration and Operations, First Aid, Rescue Techniques, Radiological Monitoring, Fire Fighting, Unexploded Ordnance Reconnaisance and Mass Feeding.

COMMUNICATIONS

Communications is another field of Civil Defense Activities in which available public funds have been utilized to improve efficiency in the public safety services as well as to prepare for the possibility of Civil Defense emergency communications needs in Maryland. It is obvious that fast and dependable communications are necessary for Civil Defense purposes. The primary network for communications is the Civil Defense—State Police Radio Network.

By this system the State Control Center at Pikesville and the Maryland Counties are linked for instantaneous communication in Civil Defense emergencies while the State Police have day-to-day use of the system for its regular operations. The State Department of Forests and Parks Radio Network, with a base station located at the State Civil Defense Control Center, provides another State-wide Radio Network which can assist in providing emergency communications at time of need.

FIRE DEPARTMENT COOPERATION

The Maryland Civil Defense Agency has cooperated with the volunteer firemen throughout the State in providing radio equipment in fire houses and on fire apparatus which is reflected in increased capability of the fire services due to the improved mobility. The Agency has provided more than 200 units of radio equipment to practically all counties in the State by assisting in obtaining and providing matching funds which have been used in the purchase and installation of the radio equipment.

The nation's largest State-wide project to test mutual aid procedures of fire departments was held in Maryland on May 26, 1957, when "Operation Flame" was conducted. More than 200 pieces of fire apparatus moved, under State coordination, to 13 "incidents" in various parts of the State.

AMATEUR RADIO OPERATORS

Amateur Radio Operators in Maryland have cooperated wholeheartedly in the organization of the Radio Amateur Civil Defense Services (RACES) at the State level, in Baltimore City and in the counties. Radio equipment has been made available at the State and County level with the aid of matching funds to implement the RACES plans.

Testing of Maryland Civil Defense operating procedures has taken place regularly during the past four years during the National Operation Alert and other State or local exercises. The National test takes the form of a Command Post Exercise and has run for varying times from 55 to 72 hours. Governor McKeldin personally has taken part in several of these exercises. Appraisal of activity at the conclusion of each exercise indicates steady progress of Civil Defense preparedness in Maryland.

WIDE EDUCATIONAL PROGRAM

Civil Defense literature in great quantities has been distributed to Marylanders in a program to keep them abreast of current developments.

A mailing list of 20,000 is now receiving the Old Line Alert, a regular publication of the Agency. Achievements of the State and Counties in Civil Defense are chronicled in this publication. The film library of the Agency has grown throughout the years. Viewers of these films have increased each year and now more than 80,000 Marylanders annually see Civil Defense films.

The State has produced a film of its own entitled "Are You Prepared" which depicts the activities of Civil Defense in Maryland. Several of the counties and Baltimore City, likewise, have produced motion picture films which show their Civil Defense units in action.

Patriotic Marylanders with their eyes turned to the sky have manned the Ground Observer Posts throughout the State for the Air Force while other of their fellow citizens stood long hours of watch at the Air Force Filter Center in Baltimore.

Constant improvements in our electronic detection equipment allowed the Air Force to place all the Observation Posts and Filter Centers on a stand-by basis on January 1, 1958.

Civil Defense is not a static program but a series of changing concepts geared to changes in modern weapons of warfare. Charged with keeping Maryland in line with current thinking are Survival Study Staffs. The State has entered into three different contracts with the Federal Government which pays the entire cost of these projects. The Maryland Survival Study Group, along with a similar one working in the District of Columbia Area, is the study and planning arm of Civil Defense.

Veterans' Commission

The Maryland Veterans' Commission with its eight strategically located offices and thirty-four itinerant locations has provided valuable assistance to Maryland veterans, their dependents and survivors. Those in need of the services of the Maryland Veterans' Commission are assured the expert assistance of trained specialists.

When their cases come before the Rating and Adjudication Boards of the Veterans Administration they are assured of excellent representation in their behalf. A constantly expanding veteran program for a constantly increasing veteran population points to a greater demand for the services of the Maryland Veterans' Commission in the years to come.

The combination of an ever-increasing veteran population and increased demands of World War I and World War II veterans has contributed to the increasing work load of the Maryland Veterans' Commission.

Advanced age and the infirmities which accompany aging has made World War I veterans eligible for, and in need of, increased Federal benefits. Further, upon the death of a veteran, benefits are due the next of kin. Widows and orphans need and receive the expert guidance of trained personnel of the Maryland Veterans' Commission. Pension for the living veteran and widow, educational benefits for the orphaned children, and hospitalization for the veteran have, along with death and burial benefits, increased and shall continue to increase.

NEW BENEFIT ASSISTANCE

Each session of Congress and each session of the Maryland General Assembly brings about changes in laws pertaining to veterans. New benefits have been provided and it is the responsibility of the Maryland Veterans' Commission not only to assist eligibles in receiving those benefits but to maintain a vigorous campaign of public information. The Maryland Veterans' Commission makes use of all mediums of public communication. Regular press releases, news to radio and television, the use of printed informational material, and personal contact through veteran, civic and fraternal organizations has helped keep our veteran population aware of the services and benefits available.

On January 1, 1958, the Maryland Veterans' Commission had active files on over 50,830 veterans in the State. The following table gives a breakdown on the number and types of services rendered to veterans or their families since January, 1951:

Disability Pension Claims	5,417
Death Pension Claims (Widow's Benefits)	1,682
Dependent Parent Claims (Parents' Benefits)	466
Insurance Claims (Nat'l. Service Life, etc.)	512
Burial Allowance Claims	1,502
Hospital & Domiciliary Applications, etc.	8,396
Power of Attorney (Required to Represent Veterans)	17,887
Duplicate Discharges	1,534
Affidavits & Notary	28,651
Consultation & Guidance, etc.	163,094
Loan Guaranty; Eligibility Certificates	856
Requests for Government Grave-Markers	740
Out-Patient Treatment (Medical & Dental)	4,768
All Others	15,478
Telephone Calls	87,590
Mail (number of pieces)	287,350

MONETARY BENEFITS RECEIVED

Since 1951, through the aid and efforts of the Commission, Maryland veterans have received a total of $9,203,295.00 in cash benefits.

It is important to understand that this amount represents first year awards only. Since many of these awards continue for years they pyramid until during the past fiscal year millions of dollars came to Maryland veterans in selected benefits.

Many recipients of these Federal awards would be of necessity forced upon the relief rolls of their counties, or the State of Maryland, were it not for these benefits.

The net savings to the people of Maryland is obvious.

The estimated distribution of Maryland Veterans in civil life, and number who now are receiving compensation or pension from the Veterans Administration Baltimore Regional Office:

W. W. I	47,000
W. W. II	240,000
Korean	47,000
Total	334,000

The War Records Division of the Maryland Historical Society

Operating under authority delegated by the Board of Public Works, the War Records Division of the Maryland Historical Society is charged with collecting, preserving and publishing data relative to Maryland's participation in World War II.

Matters of policy have been determined by a committee of Society members. The group agreed that, in addition to making the records available to the public, the Division should publish four volumes listing the State's military, industrial and agricultural contributions to the war, the home front volunteer services of its citizens, and a Gold Star Honor Roll of those who died in their nation's service.

By January 1951, the beginning date of this report, the program of collecting data was at its peak, and one volume, "Maryland In World War II—Military Participation" was in print. During 1951 a second volume, "Maryland In World War II—Industry and Agriculture" was published.

At the request of the Board of Public Works the Division then edited, put through the press and distributed histories of two Maryland military units: "The History of the 110th Field Artillery" (1953) by Col. John P. Cooper, Jr., and "History of the 175th Infantry" (1955) by James Fitzgerald Brewer.

Reverting to its original program, the Division issued "Maryland In World War II—Gold Star Honor Roll," in 1956. A final volume titled "Maryland in World War II—Home Front Volunteer Services" was published May 1, 1958.

By direction of the Board of Public Works a free copy of each publication of the Division is given to all tax supported libraries and to schools at the secondary level or above. The remaining copies are sold and the proceeds deposited in accordance with directions from the Office of the Comptroller.

In June 1955 the Division learned that carbon copies of the discharges and separations from service of over 200,000 Maryland World War II veterans were in the custody of the Selective Service Records Depot and were scheduled for imminent maceration. Prompt action by the Board of Public Works enabled the Division to obtain these records which are frequently consulted by veterans, veterans' survivors, military units, veterans' organizations and law enforcement agencies. This action was, undoubtedly, a very valuable public service.

War Memorial Commission

This Commission, composed of ten members—five appointed by the Governor and five appointed by the Mayor of Baltimore City—directs and controls the preservation of the War Memorial Building and the fronting Plaza.

The War Memorial was designed as a place of meeting for all patriotic and ex-service organizations, a depository for trophies of wars in which our Country has engaged and as a tribute to those Marylanders who gave their lives and services to their homeland.

At all times both the Building and the Plaza are available for any functions of those Veterans Organizations, their Posts and Auxiliaries.

The Commission supervises all activities pertaining to Veterans Day, United Nations Day and many other celebrations of veteran activities.

At Christmas time the Plaza is the site of the official Municipal Christmas Tree, symbolic of the festive season.

Hall of Records

Our most significant accomplishment has been the initiation and development of a records management service for State and local agencies of government. The proliferation of governmental records in our time, especially during the last twenty-five years, has created a crisis of the first order in the procedures of government; it has become necessary to provide through some central service agency for the orderly retention no less than the orderly disposal of records.

During the period covered by this report, we have established controls over 2,660 separate record series of State, county, bicounty and municipal agencies. Approximately 40,000 cubic feet of unnecessary records have been destroyed; considerable space has been saved by microfilming six and one-half million images of State records and 4,167 reels of insurance microfilm copies have been assembled in our building.

This department is without doubt the most fully developed records management service of any of the states; it lacks only central storage depositories for records which must be maintained for a given period but which have little current usage, and this deficiency will be remedied by the acquisition of record centers in the two new State office buildings.

PUBLICATION PROGRAM PROGRESS

The publication program has prospered during this period. The department has issued two analyses of index holdings and four full-length books, all designed to make the records more easily available. It has also published six annual reports to the Hall of Records Commission. Special pride is reflected in the four editions of the Maryland Manual which have come from the press in this short span of years. Each edition has been thoroughly revised, and the Manual has become, for the first time, the authoritative, trustworthy work which it was intended to be.

The store of useful historical and administrative material has grown enormously. We have accessioned 5,857 volumes and 608 cubic feet of carefully selected records. We began to collect publications of State agencies, commissions, and boards; and we now have an excellent collection. This group of materials is especially useful to new commissions and to the General Assembly; it contains 2,400 printed and processed items plus 30,000 pages of rare items available only on microfilm.

We have also gained about fifteen hundred printed works for our small library of Maryland history. As a further aid to the use of our records we have continued to collect and prepare indexes, catalogues and calendars. The growth in this collection of finding aids during the last seven years has been primarily in the field of county and church records where our holdings of records have also shown the most significant increase.

RISE IN SERVICES

The demand for services has increased exactly in proportion to the strengthening of our resources. The number of visitors has grown from 1,183 in 1952 to 1,502 in 1957; the number of documents circulated, from 7,600 to 9,714; the number of letters of inquiry answered, from 1,190 to 1,480. The number of photostatic copies required has increased fourfold, the number of projection prints, threefold.

To maintain our materials—almost all of them unique—in good condition, we have laminated approximately 187,000 pages and bound over three hundred record volumes. We have added to our repair room resources a valuable set of binding tools, and to the photographic department several microfilm readers, a continuous-process photostatic camera, a rotary microfilm camera with automatic feeder, a portable Model E microfilmer and much other supplementary equipment.

The Hall of Records offers other services which cannot be evaluated by figures. Lacking any other historical agency, the State government and the citizens of the State rely on this department for every sort of historical aid in the preparation of lawsuits, the reconstruction of public buildings and private houses, the planning of memorials, celebrations and dedications. Every effort is made to be of service to the General Assembly for everything from the provision of historical data to the microfilming of its proceedings at the end of each legislative day. Moreover, for the convenience of the General Assembly we are open six days each week, including holidays, during its sessions, and throughout the rest of the year we are open on six days of the week, exclusive of national holidays, for the convenience of the general public.

DUE

PRINTED IN U.S.A.